D0115443

National
Opera
Guide

5

La Traviata
Verdi

Josephine Barstow as Violetta and John Brecknock as Alfredo in the 1973 ENO production by John Copley.

Preface

English National Opera Guides are companions to opera in performance. They contain articles and illustrations relevant to any production as well as those mounted by English National Opera. Of interest to all opera-lovers, also, is the complete original libretto of the opera, side by side with an English translation. There are many reasons why sung words may not be clearly distinguishable, whatever the language and however excellent the performance. The composer may have set several lines of text together, for instance, or he may have demanded an orchestral sound through which no voice could clearly articulate. ENO Guides give English readers the opportunity to know a libretto in advance and so greatly increase their understanding and enjoyment of performances whether live, broadcast or recorded.

ENO is very grateful to British Olivetti Limited for sponsoring this Guide to *La Traviata*, as part of its wide-ranging programme of support for the arts. Such sponsorship is an indication of a steadily growing public interest in opera, and we hope the Guides will prove useful to new and experienced opera-lovers alike. An audience which knows what to look and listen for — one that demands a high standard of performance and recognises it when it is achieved — is our best support and, of course, an assurance for the future of opera in the English-speaking world.

Nicholas John
Editor

5

La Traviata

Giuseppe Verdi

English National Opera Guides Series Editor:
Nicholas John

This Guide is sponsored by British Olivetti Limited

John Calder · London
Riverrun Press · New York

First published in Great Britain, 1981, by
John Calder (Publishers) Ltd, 18 Brewer Street,
London W1R 4AS

and

First published in the U.S.A., 1981, by
Riverrun Press Inc.,
1170 Broadway
New York, NY 10001

Second impression 1989

BRITISH LIBRARY CATALOGUING IN PUBLICATION DATA
La Traviata — (English National Opera Guides; 5)
    1. Verdi, Giuseppe. Traviata
    2. Operas — Librettos
    I. John, Nicholas   II. Verdi, Giuseppe
III. Piave, Francesco Maria   IV. Series
    782.1'092'4   ML410.V4

ISBN 0-7145-3848-5

LIBRARY OF CONGRESS CATALOGING IN PUBLICATION DATA is available

Typeset in Plantin by Maggie Spooner Typesetting, London
Printed in Great Britain by The Camelot Press, Southampton.

Contents

List of Illustrations

Introduction

Nicholas John

Verdi's eighteenth opera is based on *The Lady of the Camellias,* a play by Alexandre Dumas the Younger which he had dramatised from his own best-selling novel published in 1848. Between 1848 and 1852 Verdi lived mainly in Paris with the soprano Giuseppina Strepponi, who was eventually to become his second wife. So he knew Parisian society from personal experience and was able to see the play in which it was so controversially portrayed as soon as the censor lifted his ban on performance in 1852.

Verdi's early operas deal with major biblical and historical subjects. In 1849, however, he composed *Luisa Miller,* based on Schiller's drama *Kabale und Liebe,* a private tragedy that does not involve the public lives of the characters. In the following year he asked the Venetian stage poet, Francesco Piave, to turn a modern domestic tragedy into a libretto for him: *Le Pasteur* by Bourgeois and Souvestre. This, which was performed as *Stiffelio* in 1850, concerns a Protestant German pastor's forgiveness of his wife's adultery. The censor demanded drastic alterations to the text for its first performance in Trieste because there were many quotations from the Bible. As a result, the story and especially the magnificent final scene were badly mutilated. Despite its failure, Verdi's high opinion of the score may be judged from his decision eight years later to re-work it as *Aroldo,* where a similar theme of adultery forgiven is set in the period of the Crusades.

Suggestions for his next opera, commissioned by La Fenice—the main theatre in Venice, where the censorship was more sympathetic than elsewhere—ranged from *Manon Lescaut* to *King Lear.* It is clear that Verdi had not come to any settled conclusion that domestic subjects were alone suitable for his operas. But he did want to break out of the restricting traditions of Italian opera—the conventional forms as well as subjects. A composer was expected to write set pieces ('numbers') which should, by convention, be handled in certain ways. The aria, for instance, was to be introduced by a *scena,* or dramatic recitative, and then to contain two parts—a lyrical passage in usually moderate tempo with a fast closing section (the cabaletta). So he wrote to one of his librettists that he no longer wanted 'the forms nearly always employed up to now' but that he wanted rather to treat the sketch for *Lear* 'in a completely new and vast manner without regard for any of the conventions'.

At this turning point in his artistic career, Verdi chose to collaborate with Piave on Victor Hugo's play *La Roi s'amuse*—banned for decades in France because it showed a reigning (16th-century) monarch to be highly immoral. The score, which he called 'a long string of duets', did indeed break many conventions. The characters, apart from the soprano heroine, Gilda, are wholly exceptional by Italian operatic standards. It was, however, a huge success and the management invited the same team to write another piece for the theatre. In the meantime, a wild and little-known Spanish drama by Gutiérrez had caught the composer's imagination to fill a commission for the 1852/3 season in Rome. *Il Trovatore* was completed by July 1852 and performed in January 1853; Piave began work on his remarkably skilful distillation of Dumas's play in November 1852 and the music of *La Traviata* was hurriedly composed for performances in April. Work on these two operas, so different in subject, thus overlapped. Devices such as the tenor's serenade off-stage (*Trovatore* Act Four; *Traviata* Act One) while the soprano holds the stage alone, or the introduction of slow, lyrical passages such as '*Ai nostri monti*' or '*Parigi, o cara*' in the climactic final scenes, illustrate their kinship. Both operas also contain set numbers which are absolutely traditional in style: '*Tacea la notte*' or '*Il balen*' in *Trovatore*, the Brindisi or '*Di Provenza il mar*' in *Traviata*. Nevertheless, *La Traviata* develops to the furthest point so far in Verdi's career the flexible word-setting for dramatic effect that broke through the 'closed forms' of Italian operatic convention. There are few such dramatically successful dialogues as that of Violetta and Alfredo in Act One, or Violetta and Germont in Act Two.

Although Verdi lost his battle to have the opera staged in contemporary dress, its shocking topicality was not lost on audiences and it was roundly condemned for immorality in many countries. *The Times* (1856) inveighed against its 'foul and hideous horrors' and no English translations of the libretto were sold. It was, of course, the character of the fallen woman (*Traviata* literally means the woman led astray) which attracted Verdi in the first place. In her, as in the character of Rigoletto, vice and virtue are combined; whereas the jester's love for his daughter redeems his utterly vicious qualities, Violetta is a courtesan called upon to be an example of noble self-sacrifice in a venal, materialistic society.

La Traviata rapidly came to vie with *Trovatore* in popularity despite the very odd mixture of period costumes in which it was performed and despite the extraordinary alterations demanded by censors and managements in different towns. (References to '*croce e delizia*'—*literally* 'cross and delight'—became 'pain and delight'; Alfredo became Ridolfo Dermont in Naples, 1855, and Rodolphe D'Orbel in Paris, 1864 — where Dr Grenville became Dr Germont!) The title page of printed scores up to 1914 set the action around 1700, and Shaw observed (1890) that every opera-goer was familiar with 'Violetta in the latest Parisian confections and Alfredo in full Louis XIV fig'! Verdi, however, never repeated this type of intimate contemporary subject. After 1853 he turned back to history, Schiller and Shakespeare for subjects and a new scale of operatic composition.

Sophie Cruvelli, the German-born soprano who created the leading role in The Sicilian Vespers in 1855. She disappeared before the première, so the newspaper headlines ran 'Where is Cruvelli?' — but she returned (from an anticipatory honeymoon with the Baron she was to marry shortly afterwards) in time to perform. (Opera Rara)

Verdi and the Singers for 'La Traviata'

Julian Budden

Paris, February 4, 1852

Deàr Sig. Marzari

Nothing could be kinder or more flattering than your letter of January 24. For the moment I cannot give you a definite reply; but if I should write for an Italian theatre I can think of nothing better than to do so for Venice, remembering the Directorate's many kindnesses shown to me last year and the enormous zeal and commitment I found in all the performers of *Rigoletto*—which were dearer to me even than the success itself, highly gratifying as that was. That said, you will understand, Sig. Presidente, that I cannot sign a contract without knowing what the company will be. Among the prima donnas you have at present Albertini is outstanding; I have never heard her personally but she has enough successes to her credit to guarantee the outcome. I imagine that you would have nothing against my writing for her, but you should lose no time in signing her up. For myself the conditions would be roughly the same as those of last year, except for a small increase in the figure.

With most profound and respectful good wishes,

I have the honour to remain (etc.)

G. Verdi

From which it will be seen that the negotiations that would lead to *La Traviata* were begun under the fairest of auspices. In Venice's Gran Teatro la Fenice policy was determined not by a single businessman-impresario as in most Italian theatres but by the so-called Presidenza, a trio of noblemen of whom Carlo Marzari was one. Verdians to a man, they had supported the composer in all his troubles with the censorship, backed his most exacting demands and had seen their efforts crowned with success. What more natural than that they should wish to follow up his latest triumph as soon as practicable? Unfortunately Augusta Albertini Baucardé, wife of the future creator of Manrico, was not available for this or for any other Verdi première. Marzari then proposed Sofia Cruvelli, a German soprano with a reputation for eccentricity, whom Verdi had declined on that account to consider for Gilda in *Rigoletto*. Since hearing her in Paris, however, he had clearly changed his mind. 'Certainly,' he wrote back, 'it would be a wonderful stroke of fortune to be able to have her at la Fenice . . . But she is engaged for London and Paris for three years with Lumley and it would be impossible to have her in Italy . . .'.

Medori has had a success in St Petersburg and I hear very good things about her. I don't think, Sig. Presidente, that you would regret making her an offer as soon as possible. If Medori is not available I think that Barbieri is still free, but between ourselves I would not advise Gazzaniga.

I wrote two highly important roles for her in *Miller* and *Stiffelio* and I was not happy with her. Besides *Rigoletto* was a terrible flop at Bergamo, the chief cause being Gazzaniga—at least that's what I gather from our friend Piave.

Therefore, Sig. Presidente, you should set about forming the company as soon as possible, and as for my part we can fix that up in a couple of words . . . .

Marianna Barbieri-Nini was the first Lucrezia in 'The Two Foscari' (1844) and Lady Macbeth (1847) of whose remarkable ugliness Giuseppina Strepponi noted, 'If she can get a husband, none of us need worry!' She was, however, a superb dramatic artist. (Opera Rara)

As the star of *Les vêpres siciliennes* (The Sicilian Vespers), Cruvelli would justify all Verdi's good opinion of her—as well as her own reputation for odd behaviour. Mention of Marianna Barbieri-Nini, the squat, unattractive heroine of *Macbeth, I due Foscari* and *Il Corsaro*, tells us clearly that at this stage of the proceedings *La dame aux camélias* could not have been under consideration. For Dumas's heroine, as Verdi would later insist, good looks were essential.

No more is heard on the subject until Verdi's return in the spring to S. Agata (the farm he had recently bought near his birthplace which was to be his home for the next 50 years). By this time the Directorate had already begun to engage the leading singers for the 1852/53 winter season. Apart from Felice Varesi, the dramatic baritone for whom he had written the roles of Macbeth and Rigoletto, only Negrini, the tenor, the future creator of Gabriele in *Simon Boccanegra*, met with Verdi's unqualified approval.

Busseto April 14, 1852

To Sig. Marzari

I hasten to reply to your esteemed letter of the 10th instant to tell you that the choice of Negrini to sing in the forthcoming carnival is excellent. As for the women, I will tell you frankly that I have very little confidence in the three you mention. I realise the many difficulties there are in finding a first rate prima donna in these times;

Fanny Salvini-Donatelli was married to a famous actor and had herself been in the straight theatre before turning to opera; she created the role of Violetta. (Opera Rara)

but you, Sig. Presidente, should do all in your power to find one who could make up the triad with the tenor and baritone and who could satisfy the high demands of the Teatro la Fenice . . .

The three women were Fanny Salvini-Donatelli, an old fashioned 'soprano d'agilità'; Marietta Alboni, Italy's leading contralto who specialised in trouser roles (Meyerbeer had adapted for her the role of Urbain in the Italian version of *Les Huguenots*) and whose phenomenal lower extension allowed her to sing Don Carlo in *Ernani* in London (1847) at the original baritone pitch; and Carolina Alaymo who in the event proved unavailable for the period required. So too did Carlo Negrini; at which point the Directorate judged it prudent to send their secretary, Guglielmo Brenna, to Busseto to confer with the composer in person. A born diplomat, on the friendliest terms with all concerned, Brenna wrote back to Marzari:

Dear Sig. Carlo

I am writing from Maestro Verdi's country house where I arrived at a bad moment, since his father is ill with a severe inflammation of the bowels and is almost at death's door. Nevertheless as far as the anxiety of the situation allowed I began discussions with Verdi on the object of my visit. . . .

Verdi would have preferred that the prima donna were Alaymo rather than Salvini Donatelli; nevertheless he will not refuse to write for the latter. Under no circumstances will he consider writing for Alboni. He says that he writes his operas with a view to their circulating and that a work composed for Alboni would not be hired out more than three times a year. Still less will he consider writing a male role for contralto. He hates transposing the sexes. Therefore there could be no question of reworking Alboni's part for tenor or baritone since in any event he would only write a female part for contralto.

The opera which he seems most readily disposed to write will probably require two women. In any case if one of the operas chosen for the season should be *Il Corsaro* two women will be needed, a prima donna and a comprimaria.

Rosina Penco impressed Verdi with her performance as Leonora in the first production of 'Il Trovatore', five months before that of 'La Traviata'. She sang the role in London in 1861. (Opera Rara)

When the contract arrived he professed himself generally satisfied with its terms. Although the subject was still unchosen he was confident that the libretto could be ready for the censorship by the end of July.

But it was not until the middle of a rainy November after subject upon subject had been considered and discarded that Piave was able to announce excitedly from S. Agata that Verdi had suddenly decided on *La dame aux camélias* and that he, Piave, had never seen him so worked up. Beyond changing the proposed title *Amore e morte* to *La Traviata* the censors made no objection. A codicil to Verdi's contract dating from October had stipulated that, should the female lead prove unsuitable for Salvini Donatelli, the management would replace her with another soprano of Verdi's choice provided they were apprised of his decision by January 15; but the date passed with no word from Verdi, who was in the throes of the first production of *Il Trovatore* in Rome. Then, at the end of January 1853, he demanded the removal of Salvini Donatelli from the title role on the strength of bad reports received. 'The only women who seem to me to be suitable are: first, Signora Penco who is singing [Leonora in *Il Trovatore*] in Rome; second, Signora Boccabadati who is singing *Rigoletto* in Bologna; and lastly Signora Piccolomini who is now singing in Pisa. Penco (the only one whom I know personally) would I think be the best. She has looks, soul (*anima*) and a good stage presence—excellent qualities for *La Traviata*.' He added that he himself was suffering from pains in the arm and that if by any chance he could not finish the opera in time, Penco could at least sing Leonora in *Il Trovatore* for them, having just created the role. Meanwhile could Piave please be given

Marietta Piccolomini, a beautiful and aristocratic soprano much admired in London, where she created the role of Violetta. (Opera Rara)

13

permission to come to S. Agata and put the finishing touches to the libretto.
It was not the first time that Verdi has proved unreasonable in the matter of casting, nor would it be the last. In 1871 he was to hold a pistol to the head of Paul Draneht, intendant of the Cairo theatre, over the allocation of the part of Amneris in *Aida*. He only gave way when he realised that his intransigence might cost Draneht his job. Once again the Fenice management yielded to the extent of trying to engage Rosina Penco, and discovered that after *Il Trovatore* in Rome she was signed up at Genoa until March 15. That being so, Marzari wrote, it was up to the composer to meet his legal obligations. The reply, written by Piave, since Verdi was still by implication unable to hold a pen, was not calculated to set the management's minds at rest: as the entire company was unworthy of the Teatro la Fenice and as it was not certain anyway that Verdi would be able to finish the opera it was no use thinking of engaging other artists; so let it be Salvini Donatelli and the rest. But (in Verdi's words) 'I declare that should the opera be given I have no hopes of its outcome; that in fact it will be a complete fiasco; the interests of the management will have been sacrificed (which could be said to be my fault) and with it my own reputation and a large sum of money due to the owner of the score. Amen'. To all this Piave appended his agreement in a post-script, adding that Verdi advised against including *Il Corsaro* in the season (as if it had not been his own idea!). He concluded, rather inconsequentially, that the opera was coming on nicely, that the first act was marvellous in point of novelty and effectiveness and that he himself felt a new man now that the reputation of the dear, good Salvini Donatelli was assured.

When the Presidenza received this an emergency meeting was convened, the upshot of which was the following directive, in which legalistic jargon gradually gives way to Venetian plain speaking:

Venice February 8, 1853
To Signore Guglielmo Brenna, Secretary to the Presidenza of the Gran Teatro la Fenice.

The Presidenza, finding itself in a state of cruel uncertainty regarding the intentions of Signor Maestro Verdi in matters pertaining to the new opera promised by him and anxiously awaited by all, directs you to proceed with all possible haste to the above-mentioned Maestro so as to obtain definite information from him and to resolve these difficulties whatever they should happen to be and howsoever they may be removed.

The letters received from Signor Piave, poet, increase rather than put an end to these perplexities; moreover as correspondence by mail is insufficiently punctual it is essential that you leave for the place where Maestro Verdi at present resides.

It is well that he has receded from his expressed wish that another singer should be substituted for Salvini Donatelli — whom neither justice nor respect for commitments entered into would allow to be set aside.

Indeed the Maestro is sufficiently convinced of this to have withdrawn his instructions to the management to that effect, but we are sorry to hear that in so doing he should express grave doubts as to the outcome of the opera, and, what is still worse, should pronounce the present company unworthy of the Teatro la Fenice.

Was he not aware since last spring when he signed the contract of their names and their qualities? And why, with his knowledge of and ability to judge their merits does he wait until this late hour to express his opinion? Does he really need mischievous and partisan reports

14

from others of an unfortunate outcome of a very doubtful opera or of a substitute-work hurriedly prepared in order to revile all these artists who moreover have begun the season with the happiest of auspices; and are they not a match for any now engaged at theatres of la Fenice's standing? Has Verdi himself so little faith in his own inspiration and his well-known skill in writing correctly for his artists that he doubts a successful outcome, which is assured both by his great genius and his recent triumphs achieved with a company which in general is little, if at all, superior to our own? Come now; the distinguished Maestro should not fall a prey to such wrong-headed notions; let him come here amongst his friends and admirers and have no fear.

We most earnestly trust that his illness will not get worse, indeed that he is already on the road to recovery; but if, Heaven forbid, this indisposition should prevent him from finishing the opera and from coming here he must be made to see in what an awkward plight his delays have placed us, and how it would be impossible to find a suitable substitute work with which to meet our many obligations . . . .

Brenna did as he was told and no more is heard from Verdi before the première (March 1853) apart from one or two snappy notes addressed to Piave. As to the outcome itself, discordant views continue to be expressed. Verdi was in no doubt that it was a fiasco and wrote as much to various friends. Recently it has been maintained that it was not a fiasco at all, or, if it was, Verdi himself deliberately brought it about. This last supposition is, of course, nonsense. Verdi was far too much the professional for that, though it is possible that his own dissatisfaction with the arrangements made (including the management's refusal to have the opera performed in contemporary dress) may have to some extent demoralised the cast. It did not, however, demoralise the orchestra, to whose conductor Verdi addressed a special note of congratulation before leaving Venice.

In fact Salvini Donatelli would appear to have acquitted herself as well as her generous build and conventional skills allowed. The first act with its brilliant concluding cabaletta was an unqualified success, and it was only later that she failed to hold the audience's attention; even so she remained sufficiently in Verdi's good graces for him to have jotted down in her 'Stammbuch' a quotation

Felice Varesi, the baritone who created Macbeth in 1847 and Rigoletto in 1851. (Opera Rara)

15

from Act Three. The real trouble seems to have come partly from the ailing Ludovico Graziani (Alfredo), on whose account the third performance had to be suspended, and surprisingly from Felice Varesi who proved incapable of sustaining the straight lyrical role of Germont. In its original form the part is indeed murderously high, but that can only be due to the composer's wish to confine Varesi to an area in which he felt comfortable. At all events, it put an end to a once fruitful collaboration as well as a friendship. With the naive egoism characteristic of so many stars, Varesi wrote to *L'Italia Musicale*, house magazine of the firm of Lucca, chief rivals to Verdi's publishers, the Casa Ricordi, complaining that *La Traviata* had failed because Verdi did not know how to make the most of his singers. The public had expected that he would write something tremendous for the protagonist of *Macbeth* and *Rigoletto*. Verdi had let him and them down.

'Either the singers for the opera or the opera for the singers' became a favourite maxim with Verdi in later life. For the Italian composers of his and earlier generations the latter proposition held good; and the directors of the Fenice theatre expected Verdi to conform to it. Since his earliest years Verdi had, however, inclined increasingly to make the opera his starting point. Having decided to write *Macbeth* for Florence in 1847 he immediately made certain of the ideal interpreter for the title role. Had he decided on *La Traviata* at the time of signing his contract he would doubtless have been able to find a Violetta to his liking. But by the time the opera had taken shape in his mind the cast had long been fixed. Evidently Verdi had gambled upon getting his own way at the last moment and lost.

Verdi in 1852, a photograph taken in Paris.

Yet the qualities demanded by Verdi for his heroine—'looks, soul and a good stage presence'—are not so hard to obtain. What he did not want was a conventional prima donna. For the opera's first revival in Venice at the Teatro S. Benedetto he was prepared to entrust the title role to a young soprano whom he had never heard, leaving the production to Piave. At the same time, while lowering Germont's part to a more normal baritone range, he lightened some of the technical demands made on the soprano. Maria Spezia, as frail as her predecessor had been robust, was never to achieve true stardom; yet her qualities were sufficient to redeem 'the fallen woman' in the eyes of the world—since when *La Traviata* has never left the repertory.

16

'La Traviata': from Real Life to Opera

Denis Arnold

Verdi's choice of *La dame aux camélias* as the subject for an opera was both original and a stroke of genius. There was no work in which he could have found a model for such an opera. Admittedly the medium affected the message. We may suspect that the heroine of the original true life story of Dumas *fils's* love affair with a courtesan was hardly acceptable as a role for an operatic diva of the 1850s; even in Dumas's novel in which he first idealises her, she is, though a woman of charm and grace, a swearing, drinking young woman who was far from the conventional heroine. Her red camellias worn on the days of the month when she was 'not available' acknowledged a physical fact not generally referred to in polite society. In the play in which Dumas took one further step from reality this meaning of the camellias has gone, along with the lewd language — and also much of the obvious enjoyment of the promiscuity in which the heroine indulges. From the play it is not a far cry to Piave's libretto, and although there are necessary cuts which may damage its delicate psychology, as Ernest Newman alleges, the courtesan now emerges as the victim of self-sacrifice which fits in well with the conventions of romantic opera. But this hitherto unknown approach to realism posed such problems that Verdi never attempted such a subject again and when the verists of the *fin-de-siècle* followed up his suggestion they vulgarised his conception.

The difficulties were, in the first place, those of a musical language. Realism involves an abandonment of at least the most improbable operatic conventions, the inevitable succession of *cavatina* and *cabaletta*, and the reliance on aria. Verdi, never a revolutionary, had yet more or less solved these problems in *Rigoletto*, with its single true full scale aria ('*Caro nome*') and its exploitation of a peculiarly subtle accompanied recitative and arioso, the result of the development of techniques known to Rossini and Donizetti where, by using the orchestra to give continuity of melody, the action could continue naturally without the protagonists singing in clear cut patterns. The strong, regular musical phrases, the constant repetition of tight, short rhythmic motives, no doubt appropriate to the heroic figures of historical drama, do not fit the bourgeois, un-heroic characters of this new style of story. A more conversational melody has to be created, for both orchestra and voice. When Verdi said that he considered *Rigoletto* his favourite from the professional point of view, he probably meant that he had succeeded in precisely this; when he declared his leanings for *La Traviata* as an amateur (a word which implies 'love' rather than technical perfection), he may well have been referring to his compromise — for there is much of the old *cavatina/cabaletta* here, though subsumed into the continuous flow of music in such a highly imaginative way that we may agree to disagree with his own assessment: for what is greater skill than the assimilation of existing, well-tried forms into something new?

Finally, there was a need for a new orchestration. Again, *Rigoletto* had lead the way. The composer who uses the low register of the clarinet and the high one of a muted double bass to convey the sinister atmosphere of the assassin's alley near the Mincio is ready for further adventures in sound. It was in *La Traviata* that these succeeded.

Amelita Galli-Curci as Violetta at the Met., where she triumphed in 1921. (Ida Cook Collection)

Act One

The Prelude to Act One shows at once a new approach to Italian opera. It is a tone picture in two parts. The opening [1], to be heard again at the beginning of Act Three when Violetta is dying, is surely an expression of the frailty of the heroine. The delicacy of the scoring is extremely beautiful, the violins divided in a way not unlike that in the overtures to Wagner's *Lohengrin* or Weber's *Euryanthe* (neither of which Verdi probably knew at this time), the dynamic markings insisting both on the quietest of tone and (by accents on weak beats of the bar) sustained sound; while the heartbreak is conveyed by the broken motif as the melody rises to the climax. The second phase has the famous melody associated with Violetta's love for Alfredo (to appear later as [16]). The dynamics again are full of *pianissimos*, with *forte* only at the moments of passion when the cellos burst twice into the *diminuendo*.

After this it comes as a shock for the curtain to go up on a party—and on brash party music [2]. The music which would normally be played by a wind band on the stage (as in *Rigoletto*) is now given to the orchestra in the pit; and soon it is plain that this is part of the building up of a 'natural' atmosphere, for the voices vie with the music as at real parties; while the tunes change from time to time in the manner of dances at balls. Against this, the characters are introduced to us—and each other: Violetta and her multitudinous guests who include her 'protector' the Baron, her friend Flora, and the young attractive Alfredo, who is introduced by one Gaston. As yet they are not strongly differentiated, and it is only as they take supper that the situation begins to emerge. The Baron is already jealous of Alfredo, who, Gaston has revealed, called at Violetta's house every day two years ago when she had been ill. When she asks the Baron to lead a toast, he refuses. She passes the invitation over to Alfredo who accepts.

The following *brindisi* [3] (or drinking song) is the first real interruption to the dance music; and yet its insertion does not seem to break up the continuity (Verdi has, in any case, finished in the wrong key so as to make the conclusion of the section indecisive). Like the Duke's *ballata* in *Rigoletto*, which arrives at the same stage in the action, the *brindisi* is a direct, memorable tune (though Verdi does not want just a brash rendering, being careful to mark the tenor's verse *'con grazia, leggerissimo'* and the decorative 'turn' figure at the end of the first full phase is *pianissimo*). But the chorus can take it up without danger and the subsequent division of the melody between Violetta and Alfredo is a natural way of showing their increasing affection. The dance music is resumed (there is now a real stage band to play a waltz [4]). Suddenly Violetta feels faint, to the alarm of her guests, most especially Alfredo. The fact that life goes on inexorably is pointed out by the sublime indifference of the band which continues playing the waltz while the lovers, now alone, have the opportunity to reveal their feelings—broken, consumptive melody for Violetta and Alfredo's ardent love shown by the gradual building up of his part into what at first seems to be an aria. '*Un dì felice*' ('I saw a vision ethereal') [5] is memorable for its insistence on a rhythmic fragment:

19

Valerie Masterson as Violetta at ENO

which is welded into a grand climax which seems vaguely familiar because it is related to the second section of the Prelude [6]; and for an unexpected turn to the minor key to express the mysterious delights of love (the comment of one writer that a Swinburnian masochism is implied in the juxtaposition of *croce e delizia — cross and delight—* is surely far from the mark).

The aria now turns into a duet [7] as Violetta replies with flirtatious *fioriture* (ornamental turns); her increasing love comes in later phrases, where falling chromatic figures convey deeper feeling. There is a duet cadenza, which is the

20

first real reminder of operatic conventions. Then Gaston returns and, with him, the insensitive world suggested by the waltz played by the stage band. Alfredo and Violetta say their farewells, and the guests depart to the opening music of the act, the stage band swallowed up by the brassy full orchestra.

At this moment we realize that there have been events but no conspicuous break in the music, no recitative, no formal aria—though plenty of good tunes. How it has been done is almost miraculous; and, such is the extended nature of the scene that to call the final stage of the party 'Stretta [a fast concluding section] dell' Introduzione Atto I', as someone (Verdi himself?) has done in the score, seems absurd. 'Introduction' indeed! We are now far into the play. Only from the singer's point of view can it be so imagined: for now comes the first true recitative and aria. Violetta is alone and muses over the events of the evening. Her recitative is so well thought out that we (and the conductor) must wonder whether the orchestra's first notes should be a dramàtic *tremolando* or a measured, quasi thematic motif (the notation could mean either). In any case the aria [9] is masterly. Its first section ('*Ah, fors'è lui*') in the minor key reveals Violetta's new found love; and second phase ('*A quell'amor*') is in fact Alfredo's proclamation of *his* love, '*Di quell'amor*' [6] in the major key as it must be, but complete with the mysterious tinge of the minor key—that juxtaposition of '*croce e delizia*' which, Swinburne or no, is the essence of the opera. The second strophe complete with cadenza is often omitted in performance. In accompanied recitative she numbers the reasons for putting aside this fantasy. With a cadenza, she tells herself to enoy her usual hedonistic life of love, and the following *cabaletta* '*Sempre libera*' ('Give me freedom') [10] would conclude the matter (and the act) in a conventional opera. But Alfredo is heard singing of his love and yet again of '*croce e delizia*' under the balcony. Violetta's mood infects this too and her brilliant *fioriture* express her feverish excitement and her frantic determination to enjoy the pleasures of life.

Act Two

Critics have noted that by cutting out the emotional development embodied in the second act of Dumas's play, where the point is made that the lovers cannot afford to live together unless the heroine continues to give herself to her rich protector, Piave and Verdi have made a rather abrupt transition to the already-achieved domesticity of their second act. But opera does not need to work in the manner of a well-made play and can assume gaps of several months in the action. Within a few bars of its opening, Act Two seems quite natural in atmosphere. The scene is a bourgeois country house near Paris, and Alfredo enters in bourgeois country clothes. After a few bars of introduction he tells us in an at first conventional accompanied recitative of his contentment, living with his beloved; the recitative moves into *arioso* for a moment of passionate expression of his delight that Violetta has also given up her past life for him; and this leads naturally into the aria '*De' miei bollenti spiriti*' ('My life was too impetuous') [11], its urgency of emotion conveyed partly by the strange orchestral accompaniment with repeated notes by bowed cellos and basses and plucked upper strings, partly by the rapid alternations of *fortes* in the tenor's upper register and *pianissimo* phrases.

The atmosphere is broken by a return to the brittle quaver figure which has been heard in the brief introduction to the act. The maid Annina comes in breathless and, in answer to his question, replies that she has been to Paris to

Maria Callas as Violetta in Visconti's production at La Scala in 1955. (Stuart-Liff Collection)

sell her mistress's horses and carriages to pay for the expensive luxury of an idyllic country life. To the brittle quavers is now added a rhythm more often associated with funeral marches, as Alfredo realises the disastrous situation and his hitherto extraordinary lack of perception; the march-like rhythm and quaver figure turn into the expression of his determination to ride to Paris to remedy the situation. His next set piece '*O mio rimorso*' ('I hate myself') is really the *cabaletta* to '*De' miei bollenti spiriti*', though it has been inserted into the action so cleverly that we hardly notice that, and it comes the nearest to the grand manner of *Il Trovatore* that is to be found in the opera, with insistent vocal motifs and military rhythms in the orchestra. When he has left, Violetta enters with Annina who explains that he has gone to Paris. There is now the first piece of extended recitative in the opera as Violetta first reads a letter from Flora inviting her to a ball (this, as we shall see, preparing the way for the next scene), an invitation Violetta is not disposed to accept. Then her manservant ushers in a man who introduces himself as Alfredo's father, Giorgio Germont, and accuses her of ruining his son, who has expressed the intention of selling his possessions. The truth is very different, she says, giving him a paper proving that it is *she* who is selling *her* property. Germont is taken aback (the orchestra underlines this with a curious short repeated phrase) but suggests that it is her guilty past that is making her do this. In a great outburst she says that it is her love for Alfredo that governs her life now. Germont realises that he must appeal to her to make a noble sacrifice. Even before he asks her to leave his son, she feels the impending disaster, as the orchestral *tremolando* makes clear. His plea opens the duet '*Pura siccome un angelo*' ('I have a daughter sent from God') [12], whereby he tells her that she is ruining the chances of marriage for Alfredo's sister. Violetta's anguished reply is given first in a kind of broken recitative as the orchestra develops an agitated figure; and the passionate ebb and flow of the argument between them is expressed by rapid changes of tonality culminating in Violetta's statement of the depth of her love for Alfredo which clearly Germont cannot understand. The shortness of phrase, and repetitiveness of the melody [13] lead into a truly expansive section '*Ah il supplizio è sì spietato*' ('Such a torment would be horrible'):

which takes Germont aback. He admits that giving up Alfredo will be a great sacrifice for her—but then pursues his case. She is now young and beautiful, but in the way of things, Alfredo is unlikely to remain in love with her as she grows older—and then what will happen? The nagging insistence of yet another short motif wears her down and eventually she gives in. She tells Germont in a most memorable, lyrical passage that he can tell his daughter that she will sacrifice herself, '*Dite alla giovine*' ('Comfort your daughter') [14]; and Germont is moved and comforts her in a melody which frequently clashes against the harmonies, Verdi miraculously drawing the two themes together as the pair grieve in their different ways. The climactic *cadenza* finished, they have to take practical steps. In recitative Germont tells her that she must tell Alfredo she does not love him—but she knows that Alfredo will just not believe her. If she leaves him he will follow. To give her courage, she asks Germont to embrace her and then she sits down to write a note to her

Rosa Ponselle made her world debut as Violetta at Covent Garden in 1931 with Gigli as Alfredo. (Ida Cook Collection)

beloved. From *arioso*, the music moves into another quasi-march rhythm as she thinks she will die, Germont trying to comfort her with the thought that she will soon forget and resume her happiness. Before Germont leaves they again embrace indicating the true emotional bond which has grown between them. The musical motif of the word 'sacrifice' underlines Violetta's mood and after Germont has gone, the rhythm provides a link into the next stage of the action. She rings for Annina to take a note to an address which surprises the maid (though we are not told it)— and the strangeness of Violetta's mood is hinted at in a hesitant, anguished melody for the clarinet. Violetta is put into confusion by Alfredo's return (the orchestral accompaniment tells us of her agitation). Alfredo is clearly baffled by the change in atmosphere and a nervously inconsequential conversation follows, in which the music never seems to develop properly. Suddenly Violetta cries out, 'Love me, Alfredo'. The melody, which is related to her expression of love in their Act One duet, '*Di quell'amor*' [6] now appears in the form we first heard it in the Prelude. '*Con passione e forza*' is the instruction—but it is brief and with a quick 'goodbye'(significantly turning to the minor key for just a single note) she runs out into the garden.

Alfredo, not surprisingly, is now completely baffled—but not particularly disturbed although the orchestra conveys the observer's sense of unease. A servant enters with Violetta's letter. Alfredo has only to read the opening to realize she has left him, and jumps to the assumption that she has returned to the luxuries provided by her old protector. His anguish is as sudden as Violetta's had been a few minutes ago (the change of key and the use of the orchestral *tutti* are both very similar) but his father, having entered from the garden, tries to comfort him, attempting to bring him to his senses by reminding him of his family home in Provence, in an expressive aria [17]. This is very consistent in tone with his patriarchal address to Violetta earlier (and if the calm, much-to-be-respected father figures seem the stuff of 19th century Italian opera, it must be said that they are still by no means uncommon in present day middle-class Italian society). Alfredo is not really convinced, the unease returns both between the strophes of the aria and at its end. He catches sight of Flora's invitation, guesses where to find Violetta and dashes off, followed by his father, to confront her.

The scene changes to Flora's mansion, the mood of the party music of Act One returns (the dance music [18] again in the pit rather than given to the stage band) and, as before, a conversation between the characters is given musical continuity in the orchestra. A ballet of fancy-dressed guests (as is suitable for a work with a French subject, since a ballet was a sine qua non at the Opéra) begins with a group of gypsies [19]. During this, Flora engages in gossip with friends. Will Violetta come (presumably with the Baron, who seems now again to be in favour) or will Alfredo, who has also been invited? The ballet resumes with Spanish bull fighters [20], much applauded by the other guests, including Flora's immediate friends. The gaiety is interrupted by the entrance of Alfredo, who is followed shortly by Violetta, on the arm of the Baron. The minor key, a shifty theme [21] played by violins and clarinets in an uncomfortable lower register, conveys the immediate unease. Violetta is taken aback on seeing Alfredo and her anguish is clear from her phrase '*Ah, perchè veni incauta?*' (It was madness to come here!) [22], the lyricism of which is strangely at odds with the tense, febrile music of the others. Alfredo insists on playing at cards for high stakes with his rival (as it seems to him), the Baron. Alfredo cleans him out, the atmosphere electric as the Baron needles him with the saying 'lucky at cards, unlucky in love'. The tension is broken

Verdi's manuscript score of the concerted finale of Act Two. (Archivio Storico Ricordi)

when they go off to supper. There is an uneasy cadence before Violetta returns followed by Alfredo. She tells him to leave at once. Alfredo believes that she thinks it might come to a duel in which the Baron might be killed, but in heroic tones expressed in another finely rhythmic melody, he sings that he does not care whether he, Alfredo, will die because he will have had his revenge. Violetta protests that it is not the Baron for whom she is afraid but him. 'Then leave with me', he sings but she cannot. To a significant and terrifying orchestral *tutti* he flings open the door of the ante-room and calls the others to hear. His accusation is made in yet another melody built from short repetitive rhythmic motifs: this woman spent her fortune on me— now I pay her back. He flings his winnings on the floor. There is a moment of pandemonium while everybody sings *velocissimo* [23]. Then his father, who has arrived unannounced, takes control. He is ashamed of his son (though since he alone knows the whole story, this patriarchal gesture is surely more than a little unjust) and is prepared to disown him. Alfredo, in a nervous motif, is shocked; Violetta '*con voce debolissima e con passione*' despairingly says that he understands nothing of her love [25]: and from these different emotions one of the greatest ensembles in Italian opera is built up, as usual in Verdi with a great melody:

surrounded by significant subsidiary figures; and Verdi, with insight and tact, dispenses with any *stretta* or vulgar working up to an artificial fast climax.

Act Three

The extraordinary and beautiful Prelude to this Act begins with the music which had begun the whole opera and is similarly scored; but after a few bars the theme is differently developed, for there is now no place for the lively, passionate love theme associated with Alfredo. All is impending death, as is revealed when the curtain rises on Violetta's bedroom. La Traviata is deeply sick and attended only by Annina. The themes of the Act's Prelude are used as the background to the conversation of mistress and maid and the doctor, who tries to cheer up Violetta with comforting words about convalescence. On the way out he reveals to Annina the truth: there is little time left. Nor remains there much money. Violetta's only comfort is the letter sent her by Giorgio Germont which she reads aloud, solo strings playing Alfredo's '*Di quell' amor*' [6] as she remembers that very first meeting. The emphasis is now surely on the first word of '*croce e delizia*'— the music breaks off suddenly. In a sepulchral voice (the instruction is Verdi's) she speaks: 'It is too late' for Alfredo's return promised in Germont's letter. She tries to get up, she looks at her withered body in the mirror and realises that death is near. She now sings her farewell to life '*Addio del passato*' ('Forever I must leave thee') [26], a remarkable aria based, as so often in Verdi, on a short motif which recurs in about every bar; and the cruellest part of her fate is that Alfredo, her love for whom is expressed in a single expansive phrase, is not here to comfort her— the oboe's echoes of her obsessive little motif convey the essence of loneliness. Then, as is supposed to happen with consumptives, she suddenly finds her strength again and begs for divine pardon on a penitent sinner. This short passage in the major key gains its musical strength by the orchestral scoring, thick at both bottom and top, the yawning gap in the middle somehow embodying the emptiness of Violetta's life:

VIOLETTA

but it is too late—the motif of the first section returns and she finishes each strophe (there are two, and to cut the second, as is sometimes done, in my opinion, ruins the proportions of the act) on a top A *un fil' di voce*—no doubt impossible for consumptives, yet extraordinarily moving.

Carnival revellers are heard outside [27] to underline that, as ever, people may be dying, but life goes on. Then, in one of the very few musically weak passages in the whole opera, Annina comes in excitedly to tell Violetta that Alfredo has arrived: the obvious 'link' passage is forgiven when he comes in and with an enormous outburst Violetta throws her arms around him. Their excitement is expressed by commonplace but effective broken chords in the orchestra. For a moment hope returns and Alfredo proposes that they should leave Paris and live together ('*Parigi, o cara*' 'Come, bid farewell to Paris for ever') [28]. Violetta sings the second strophe and then they join together—but the fragility of their future prospects is underlined by a curious chromatic figure [28a] which keeps recurring, '*de' corsi affani*' ('Your grief will vanish'), and is developed into the final cadenza. Realism returns, and in another weak musical link, Violetta suddenly becomes pale and Alfredo sends Annina to fetch the doctor. There is a thunderous chord on the brass and Violetta realises that if Alfredo's return cannot revive her, she is indeed doomed. The lovers sing another duet of a quite different kind ('*Gran dio! morir sì giovine*' 'Ah! oh God, to die when I'm so young') [29], the effect of which is gained largely by the way that the *forte* opening rapidly dies away to *pianissimo* and that loud and soft bars are frequently juxtaposed. There is one more climax as Violetta has a further consumptive burst of energy. Then all is lost. Germont arrives, though his words of comfort that he now considers her as his daughter, hardly seem enough. The funereal chords which often convey a sense of doom in Verdi (as in the 'Miserere' scene of *Il Trovatore*) usher in the last stage, as all the characters are now present. Violetta's heroic nature (as opposed to what could have been made into one of pathos—as in Puccini's similar consumptive in *La Bohème*) is made still clearer by her hope that Alfredo will find a suitable bride [30]. Hers is a positive, not just a passive love. She suddenly revives, to a wild version of '*Di quell' amor*' even ending on a top B flat; then she falls back dead, leaving the others to grieve.

Alexandre Dumas the Younger and 'La dame aux camélias'

April FitzLyon

On February 2, 1852, Alexandre Dumas the Younger's play *La dame aux camélias* was produced at the Vaudeville Theatre in Paris. It was an immediate success, made Dumas's name—he was twenty-seven—and became one of the most popular French plays of the 19th century. It was a landmark in the French theatre for several reasons: it was one of the first dramas to take contemporary life as its theme; it was one of the first plays to show a modern—as opposed to historical—courtesan in a sympathetic light; finally, it was well-known that much of the play was true. Dumas *fils* had already published a novel of the same name in 1848, and had not concealed the fact that it was autobiographical, based on his own love-affair with the courtesan Marie Duplessis, who had died of consumption in 1847. Many people in the first-night audience had known her, a few even figured as minor characters in the play; certainly everyone knew all about her, for her life and death had been subjects dear to journalists, men about town, and everyone interested in gossip—in other words, all Paris. People still remembered Marie Duplessis's frequent appearances in a box at the theatre, when she was the cynosure of all eyes; they remembered her smart blue coupé, drawn by magnificent English thoroughbreds, in which she used to drive to the Bois de Boulogne. They remembered, too, the auction held in her apartment after her death to pay off her numerous creditors, when crowds of people, Dickens amongst them, had gone to gape at the elegance and luxury in which a courtesan had lived, and to speculate about the scenes which had taken place against that sumptuous décor.

Marie Duplessis—her real name was Alphonsine Plessis—was a peasant girl from Normandy. She had not come from a good home: her grandmother had been half beggar, half prostitute; her father was ill-natured, vicious, hard and debauched; his wife had left him, abandoning her two daughters. Alphonsine's father is said to have sold her to some gypsies; at any rate, when she was about fourteen she turned up in Paris, starving, dirty and in rags. Within a relatively short time she became the best-dressed woman in Paris, a trend-setter, a celebrity.

Alphonsine's progress from rags to riches was, for the epoch, classical. At first she eked out a living as a *grisette*. A *grisette* was a Parisian girl who worked in 'clean' trades: dressmaking, sewing, embroidery, braiding, flowers. Since *grisettes* were very badly paid, they were often, but not always, of easy virtue. Mimi, in Murger's *Scènes de la vie de bohème* (1849) and Puccini's opera, was a *grisette*. Alphonsine's first love-affairs may have been, like Mimi's, with poor students, but they were probably more sordid. Eventually she found a restaurant-keeper who set her up in a modest way in a little flat. But her extraordinary beauty soon caught the eye of a rich young nobleman—the Comte de Guiche, later Duc de Gramont, then aged twenty—and from then on she was launched on her career. She was kept in luxury by a number of rich lovers, mostly members of the newly-founded Jockey Club, the lions and dandies of Parisian society.

Alphonsine's most substantial bills—and they were very substantial indeed—were paid by Count Gustav Stackelberg, a retired Russian diplomat, who was then eighty years old. Three of Stackelberg's daughters had recently died young of consumption; it is said that he was so struck by Alphonsine's

Eugénie Doche the beautiful actress who created the role of Marguerite Gautier in 1852. Dumas said, 'She lacked nothing – youth, brilliance, beauty, talent . . . It was as though when she played the role, she had written it'. (Drawing by Vincent Vidal in a private collection)

likeness to one of them, and by the fact that she suffered from the same disease, that he offered to keep her in luxury, with no strings attached. Strange though this story may seem, usually reliable sources vouch for its truth; but Dumas *fils* maintained that the Count's motives were less disinterested. Stackelberg occasionally accompanied Marie Duplessis, as Alphonsine Plessis now called herself, to the theatre; he does not seem to have objected too much to her many lovers.

During the first half of the 19th century courtesans usually came from *le demi-monde*, to which neither Marie Duplessis, nor the later courtesans of the Second Empire, ever belonged. Since Dumas *fils* himself invented the expression after Marie's death in his play *Le Demi-Monde* (1855), and since he rightly foresaw that it would be misinterpreted, here is his own definition: 'Let us establish, for dictionaries of the future, that the *Demi-Monde* does not, as people believe and say in print, represent the mob of courtesans, but the group of society people who have come down in the world. Not everyone who wants to belong to the *Demi-Monde* can do so.' Society women who, for some reason—an indiscreet love affair, an illegitimate child—were no longer accepted by their peers, formed the *demi-monde*; their manners were acceptable, but their morals were not. These women were often very short of money and, either from poverty or inclination, sometimes became courtesans. Since they were educated women, from the same social set as the men who frequented them, they could provide much more than sex; they could entertain and amuse, arrange elegant parties, and provide intelligent companionship. The *demi-monde* was a refined, though permissive, society.

Despite her humble origins, Marie Duplessis belonged to this tradition of refined and intelligent courtesans; she certainly did not resemble the courtesans of the Second Empire, coarse harpies such as Cora Pearl. Unlike them, she appears to have been sensitive, modest and intuitive, to have had what Liszt described as 'an enchanting nature', to have had a heart. Unlike them, she was never responsible for scandals, debts, suicides. She had a natural refinement and distinction; and she had good taste, both in appearance and behaviour. When she arrived in Paris she could only just sign her name; but she soon learned to write correctly, to ride, to dance, and play the piano, to behave like a great lady. Her library was quite extensive: it consisted mainly of the Romantics—Dumas *père*, Lamartine, Musset, Walter Scott—but also included Molière, Cervantes and, significantly, Prévost's *Manon Lescaut* (1731), which plays a prominent part in the novel of Dumas *fils*.

Above all, Marie Duplessis learned to talk well, and this was perhaps her principal charm—men enjoyed her company. Jules Janin witnessed her first meeting with Liszt, in a theatre; Liszt was enthralled by her conversation, and they talked throughout a whole act of the play. 'No coarse expression ever passed her lips,' said an Englishman who knew her. 'Lola Montès could not make friends, Alphonsine Plessis could not make enemies.' But telling the truth was not her strong point; she used to say: 'Lying keeps the teeth white'.

Despite her way of life, Marie Duplessis retained a capacity for feeling and an innocence rare in her profession, which gave her an added piquancy. 'She had been a *grisette*,' said Dumas, 'that is why she still had a heart'. Liszt went further: 'The habit of what one calls (and perhaps is) corrupting never touched her heart'. She was the personification of the Romantic heroine: thin, pale, with large dark eyes; she was melancholy, and suffered from *ennui*, Musset's *mal du siècle*. Above all she bore what was, ever since *Werther*, the greatest Romantic distinction: she was marked in the prime of youth by the certainty of an early death.

'I shan't live,' she told Liszt. 'I'm an odd sort of girl, and I won't be able to hold on to this life, which I don't know how to lead, and which I don't know how to bear, either. Take me, take me away wherever you like; I won't be in your way, I sleep all day, in the evening you'll let me go to the theatre, and at night you'll do what you like with me.' Liszt did contemplate taking her to Constantinople, but nothing came of it. He was profoundly moved by her death, and said that, had he been in Paris when she died, he would have had his 'quarter of an hour as Des Grieux'.

Dumas *fils* met Marie Duplessis in 1844. They were both twenty years old; but whereas Marie had already reached the summit of her career, Alexandre had not yet published anything, and was merely the son of a famous father. The story of their meeting is exactly retold in Dumas's novel: Dumas figures as Armand Duval (Alfredo Germont in the opera), and Marie as Marguerite Gautier (Violetta Valery in the opera). The course of their love-affair is described in the novel with many details and subsidiary characters taken from real life; the play is necessarily more schematic, the opera even more so. 'However', wrote Dumas, 'Marie Duplessis did not have all the pathetic adventures which I ascribe to Marguerite Gautier, but she wanted nothing better than to have them. If she did not sacrifice anything to Armand, it is because Armand did not wish her to. To her great regret, she was only able to play the first and second acts of the drama'.

There are two important incidents in the drama which did not occur in real life. Firstly, Dumas *père* did not intervene in the love-affair, and his character in no way resembled that of Duval *père* who, in the fictions, speaks for conventional morality. That was not at all the line of the author of *The Count of Monte Cristo*, who was an exuberant sensualist and *bon vivant*. The second important difference is that Dumas *fils* did not return in time to have a death-bed reconciliation with his mistress, as Duval does in the stage version. The end of the story in real life was rather different.

About a year before her death, Marie Duplessis went to London with one of her protectors of long standing, the Vicomte Edouard de Perregaux. They were married in Kensington Register Office in February, 1846, and then returned to France. Both seem to have regretted this marriage, which was anyway probably not legally valid in France. They never lived together as husband and wife, and Marie did not use her husband's name, although she did sometimes use his title and his coat of arms. She died of consumption a fortnight after her twenty-third birthday. Of the many men who had been her friends or lovers, only her husband and, perhaps, old Count Stackelberg attended her funeral. Dumas was abroad at the time; when he heard the news he hurried back to Paris and, overwhelmed with remorse and nostalgia, wrote his novel in a few days. He probably was present, with Perregaux, when her body was later exhumed in order to be reburied elsewhere; this grizzly scene is described in detail in his novel. Marie Duplessis became something of a cult figure; for many years after her death people used to deposit camellias on her grave.

The title of the novel and the play was Dumas's own invention. Marie Duplessis was never referred to as '*la dame aux camélias*' during her lifetime. But she did have a predilection for those flowers, and almost always wore or carried them, partly because they were very expensive, and she loved everything expensive, but mainly because they have no scent—scent made her feel faint. Dumas may have derived his title from the nickname of a certain Lautour-Mézeray, who was known as '*l'homme au camélia*'; he was a dandy, who never went out without a camellia in his button-hole, and is reputed to have spent over 50,000 francs on this whim.

Later, Dumas *fils* turned his novel into a play. At first it was banned by the censor; but it was finally produced after the accession of Napoleon III, thanks to his half-brother, the Duc de Morny. Although *La dame aux camélias* was a box-office success from the first, it did arouse a good deal of controversy. Many people felt that it was a glorification of vice, the product of a permissive society; others, more perceptive, discerned in it in embryo the moralising element which was soon to become an integral part of all the work of Dumas *fils*; but the majority accepted it simply as a moving human story.

In *La dame aux camélias*, which is not typical of his work as a whole, Dumas *fils* for once outstripped his famous father, and created a play which has stood the test of time. It has done so partly because in it Dumas *fils* expressed a deeply-felt personal experience; but it lives mainly because in the part of Marguerite Gautier he created a magnificent opportunity for a great dramatic actress. Among the many great actresses from various countries who seized that opportunity were: Madame Doche (the first Marguerite), Sarah Bernhardt, Eleonora Duse, Ludmilla Pitoëff, and Edwige Feuillière (Paris, 1937, London, 1955). Amongst many famous productions, there was one by Meyerhold (1935). It was a very popular part of the silent cinema—there were eleven versions between 1907 and 1927, including one by Sarah Bernhardt (1911). On the screen the part was played by Yvonne Printemps (1934) and Garbo (*Camille*, 1937) among many others. Mauro Bolognini's version (1981) with Isabelle Huppert as Marguerite, is the twenty-third film to be based on Dumas's play.

At the end of the first performance of his play Dumas's friends asked him if he was going on to a party to celebrate his success. He replied that he was not, as he was spending the evening with a lady; he then went to have a quiet supper with his mother. This anecdote contains the key to Dumas's life and work, and particularly to his relationship with Marie Duplessis; for he was illegitimate, and the difficulties both he and his mother had had as a result had marked him profoundly.

Dumas's mother, Catherine Labay, who had also been a *grisette*, had lived with Dumas *père* when he first came to Paris, twenty-one years old, and quite unknown. When he became famous, he abandoned her; but he recognised his son, with whom he was very friendly, despite the difference in their characters. Catherine Labay was a virtuous and hard-working woman, whose son adored her. He had seen what she had suffered on his behalf, and he himself had suffered taunts at school about his illegitimacy. His mother's difficult life had made him able to see the woman's point of view better than most men of his time, and had made his relationship with Marie different to the relationships she usually had with men. Dumas was sympathetic to women who, at that time, could barely earn a decent living without resorting to prostitution; he was sympathetic to the predicament of illegitimate children; and he was shocked by the callous treatment women often received from men. He campaigned all his life against these ills, and in this respect can be called a pioneer of women's liberation—he was the first to use the word '*feministe*' (in 1872).

But Dumas was far from supporting feminism in all its aspects. As he grew older, and society under Napoleon III became ever more permissive, he became an ever more intransigent moralist. He wished to defend the family and family life, which he himself had never had. He waged war on adultery in any form for any reason, and even maintained that a husband could and should kill an adulterous wife. All this in theory; Dumas was himself an adulterer, and had an illegitimate child. Like many moralists, he did not practise what he preached. Many of his ideas were far-fetched, but some were not, and his numerous writings on illegitimacy and the problems of unmarried mothers did much to change public opinion and thus, eventually, French legislation. Dumas's preface to the 1868 edition of *La dame aux camélias* is a passionate defence of 'fallen' women, and an attack on 'respectable' marriages for money or position, which he considered, as Tolstoy did, to be another form of prostitution.

The first performance of Dumas's play coincided with the birth of the Second Empire, an epoch to which Marie Duplessis had never belonged, and which represented everything which Dumas *fils* deplored. Under Napoleon III's despotic regime, which silenced public opinion and took all political initiative away from the French people, the nation, encouraged by the court, gave itself up to money-making and the pursuit of pleasure. It was an affluent, empty and cynical society. Paris became what it had never been before, but what it still remains in the imagination of some foreigners: the world centre for night life and sexual permissiveness. Dumas himself laid the blame for this on the newly-invented railways, which had made access to Paris easier for provincial Frenchmen and foreigners.

Marie Duplessis, with her melancholy *ennui*, her love of poetry, and her romantic belief in the possibility of love, would have had no place in the Second Empire; she belonged rather to the Romanticism of 1830. In 1868 Dumas himself said that his play could not have been written then. 'Not only would it no longer be true, it would no longer be possible.' By then men no longer expected companionship, culture or refinement from courtesans, who had become merely expensive prostitutes, conspicuous symbols of affluence.

Beniamino Gigli who sang Alfredo regularly at Covent Garden until 1939, and at the Met..

An Introduction to the Libretto

Nicholas John

Any comparison of Piave's libretto with the play will show how much he preserved of what was admired in Dumas's work. Contemporaries used to the clichés of Romanticism noted the play's 'simplicité' and 'fraîcheur': it did not depend on improbable coincidences, the characters were not stereotyped, the language was realistic. Piave moulded the unusually informal sequence of scenes that make up the play's five acts into four scenes, concentrating on three principal characters. In these he kept closely to the characterisation (although he changed the names) and directly translated whole passages into Italian verse.

Piave differs most from Dumas in the first act. His opening scene nevertheless captures the spontaneous gaiety of the original. Dumas had to add a song here because the licence of one of the theatres, where he hoped the play would be accepted, demanded that *couplets* should be included at all performances. The dance was a polka, the most fashionable dance in Paris in the 1840s. Piave took trouble to ensure (by his late arrivals, the *brindisi* and the general surprise that there will be dancing) that Violetta's reception, although much larger than Marguerite's intimate supper party, was not at all formal. Her delight in the pleasures of the moment remains an essential part of her charm.

Dumas made a point of Marguerite's plain-speaking when she meets Armand. But when Armand talks of love his language is poetic. '*Aimez moi*', says Marguerite, '*comme un bon ami...*'. To which Armand romantically replies, '*Voulez-vous être aimée... d'un amour profond, éternel?*' Carried away by an unexpected new emotion she invites him to return when the flower she has given him has faded — '*l'espace d'un soir ou d'un matin*' — a line which has been compared to Malherbe: '*Et rose elle a vecu ce que vivent les roses, l'espace d'un matin*'.

Dumas's act ends in laughter as the guests make fun of the long *tête-à-tête* in a raucous peasant wedding chorus. Piave collected miscellaneous epigrams from the act ('*Ce qui me soutient, c'est la vie fiévreuse que je mène*', '*Puisque j'ai à vivre moins longtemps que les autres, il faut bien que je vive plus vite*') for Violetta's *scena*, inspired by Marguerite's self-questioning soliloquy in the second act. Piave otherwise eliminated this act, in which (four days after meeting him) Marguerite makes practical arrangements for a country retreat with Armand.

The play's third act is set in Auteuil, which is now in the 16th arrondissement of Paris and was then a fashionable suburb. Dumas probably relocated it from Bougival (10 miles from Paris) where it is in the novel, in order to make the quick journeys to Paris more credible on the stage. Marguerite's interview with Duval — the pivotal scene of both play and opera — is almost directly translated into the libretto. Verdi matched Duval's stiff language with four-square musical forms. Roger Clark notes (in his introduction to the play) that the sentiments, expressed here by Dumas for the first time, were to be repeated 'almost *ad nauseam*' in his later plays. The contrasting tragic lyricism of Marguerite's replies may be illustrated by the lines:

Ainsi, quoi qu'elle fasse, la créature tombée ne se relevera jamais!
Dieu lui pardonnera peut-être, mais le monde sera inflexible!

The act ends with Armand's angry cry when he reads Marguerite's letter, and his father's embrace; the next act takes place a month later. Although his letter will be read aloud in the final act, Duval does not reappear. By introducing him into other scenes so as to tighten the dramatic conflict, Piave rather strained the credibility of the plot but enabled Verdi to achieve unforgettable, if melodramatic, effects.

Apart from the fancy-dress choruses, the libretto follows the fourth act of the play closely until Duval's unexpected arrival. Violetta, unlike Marguerite, does not, however, explain that she is late because she has come from *La Favorita* at the opera — a remark which gives Armand an opportunity to comment that that is another story of a woman faithless to her lover. (He has pointedly compared their relationship to *Manon Lescaut* a number of times.) Dumas closes the act with the Baron's challenge. The opera's final act differs in some interesting details but not essentials: the progress of her illness is similarly charted, the carnival (it is New Year's Day) is observed and the religious overtones are retained. The last lines of the play are:

> Dors en paix, Marguerite! il te sera beaucoup pardonnée parce que
> tu as beaucoup aimée.

It may be regretted that the character of Prudence Duvernoy, an older woman who interests herself in Marguerite's affairs, should have been eliminated from the libretto. Some of Marguerite's soliloquy (which inspired '*E strano!*') was, in the novel, Prudence's exposition to Armand of the true situation. ('Women like that imagine that they will be loved but not that they will love.) Violetta's generosity to the poor in the last act — which is surely rather thoughtless to her faithful Annina—was originally a scene where Prudence borrowed almost half Marguerite's remaining funds to buy presents. Dumas had been even more explicit about her financial difficulties in the novel: Marguerite's possessions were security for her debts and she had scarcely any money, even for medicines, because nothing could be sold. 'You would not believe amidst what luxury Madame is dying', wrote the maid to Armand, pointing disapprovingly at Prudence's behaviour. In short, Prudence reminds us of practical and mercenary aspects of Marguerite's character which did not interest Verdi.

La dame aux camélias has been well described as the 'bourgeois flower of romanticism' (Ghéon). Dumas observed Armand's love and the romantic idyll of a country retreat with an unsentimental eye. Courtesans of previous centuries had been portrayed on the stage in Romantic drama (Victor Hugo's *Marion Delorme* (1831), for example). Balzac's novel *Splendeurs et misères des courtisanes* (1843) depicts the heroine as a victim of a ruthless society. Dumas showed a contemporary courtesan taking practical steps to change her life. Her capacity for self-sacrifice contrasts with the selfishness of both disreputable Prudence and respectable Duval, and her passionate sincerity is all the more appealing because she knows that society will not allow her to forget her past. She is unsentimentally aware of the reasons why she will never enjoy the new life for which she longs. Verdi later considered Gemma Bellincioni an outstanding interpreter of the role. Perhaps she brought to it a flavour of those *verismo* roles she created and for which she was famous —Santuzza, rejected by the Church and the villagers because her lover betrayed her, in *Cavalleria Rusticana*; and the tormented heroine of Giordano's *Fedora*, whose happy marriage in an idyllic country retreat is shattered by forces she set in motion years before.

Thematic Guide

Many of the themes from the opera have been identified in the articles by numbers in square brackets, which refer to the themes set out on these pages. The themes are also identified by the numbers in brackets at the corresponding points in the libretto, so that the words can be related to the musical themes.

[1] Adagio *ppp*

[2] Allegro brillantissimo e molto vivace *p*

[3] *Brindisi*/ALFREDO
Allegretto *con grazia leggerissimo* *p*

Be hap - py, be hap - py and raise your glass with me
Li - bia - mo, li - bia - mo ne' lie - ti ca - li - ci,

[4] Allegro brillante *p*

[5] ALFREDO.
Andantino *p*

I saw a vi - sion e - the - re - al glit - t'ring
Un di fe - li - ce, e - te - re - a mi ba - le -

there be - fore me
na - ste in - nan - te,

37

Andantino

Ah   it   is   love   and   love   is   our de - sti - ny
Di   quel - l'a - mor,   quel - l'a - mor   ch'e pal - pi - to

[7] VIOLETTA

Andantino

This   is   all   far   too   se - ri - ous, friendship is all I off - er
Ah se ciò è ver, fug - gi - te - mi! So - lo_a - mi - sta - de_jo v'of - fro;

[8] CHORUS

Allegro vivo

We pre - sent - our - selves be - fore -   you, what a
Si ri - de - sta_in ciel l'au - ro -   ra, e ne'è

splen - did - night of   fea - - - sting
for - za   di   par - ti - - - re

[9] VIOLETTA

Andantino

Is   he   the   one   I   dream   a - bout?
Ah, for - s'è lui che l'a - ni - ma

Hi - ding my tears in   laugh - ter
So - lin - ga ne' tu -   mul - ti,

[10] VIOLETTA

Allegro brillante

Give - me free - dom to   be hap - py all my
Sem - pre li - be - ra   deg - g'i - o fol - leg -

life   en - joy - ing, en - joy - ing!
gia - re di gio - ja_in gio - ja!

38

Andante

My life was too im - pe - tu - ous
De' miei bol - len - ti spi - ri - ti

[12] **GERMONT**

Allegro moderato   *dolcissimo*

I have a daugh - ter sent from God.
Pu - ra sic - co - me un an - ge - lo,

[13] **VIOLETTA**

Vivacissimo

Do you rea - lise I a - dore - him, and I
Non sa - pe - te qua - le af - fet - to vi - vo, im -

live my whole life for him?
men - so m'ar - de in pet - to?

[14] **VIOLETTA**

Andantino cantabile

Com - fort your dau - ghter so pure, and love - ly,
Di - te al - la gio - vi - ne sì bel - la e pu - ra,

[15]   [16] **VIOLETTA**

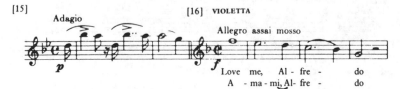

Adagio   Allegro assai mosso

Love me, Al - fre - do
A - ma - mi, Al - fre - do

[17] **GERMONT**

Andante piuttosto mosso

In Pro - vence your na - tive land, we still long for your re - turn,
Di Pro - ven - za il mar, il suol, chi dal cor ti can - cel - lò?

[18]

Allegro brillante

39

[19] CHORUS

Allegro moderato

We're gi - psy for - tune tell - ers: per - mit us to sa - lute you.
Noi sia - mo zin - ga - rel - le ve - nu - te da lon - ta - no.

[20] CHORUS

Allegro assai vivo

Here's Pi - quil - lo, strong and hand - some,
E Pi - quil - lo un bel ga - gliar - do

[21]

Allegretto agitato

[22] VIOLETTA

Allegro agitato

It was mad - ness to come here! Dear God, I
Ah, per - chè ven - ni in - cau - ta? Pie - tà, gran

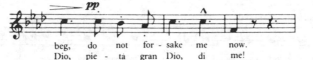

beg, do not for - sake me now.
Dio, pie - tà gran Dio, di me!

[23] CHORUS

Velocissimo unisono

You have de - stroyed her, our sen - ses are reel - ing.
Oh, in - fa - mia or - ri - bi - le tu com - met - te - sti!

[24] CHORUS

Largo

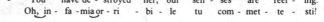

Oh poor Vio - let - ta, come dry your eyes.
O quan - to pe - ni! ma pur fa cor.

[25] VIOLETTA

Largo

Al - fre - do, Al fre - do, you hate and scorn me, you do not
Al - fre - do, Al fre - do, di que - sto co - re non puoi com-

re - a - lise   the   bit - ter   sto - ry.
pren - de - re   tut - to   l'a - mo - re.

[26] VIOLETTA

Andante mosso

I've lost you   hap- py daydreams: The   past is   all   ov - er.
Ad - di - o   del pas - sa - to,   bei   so - gni   ri -   den - ti.

[27] CHORUS

Allegro vivacissimo

Hail   to the   car - ni - val's four - foot - ed mas - ter.
Lar - go al qua - dru - pe - de   sir del - la fe - sta.

[28] ALFREDO

Andante mosso

Come   bid fare - well   to   Pa - ris for - e - ver,
Pa - ri - gi, o ca -   ra,   noi   las - sce - re - mo,

[28a]

[29] VIOLETTA

Allegro

Oh God, to   die when I'm   so young and af - ter   so much sor - row!
Gran dio! mo - rir   si gio - vi - ne,   io che   pe - na - to ho tan - to!

[30] VIOLETTA

Andante

I   see   a   pure   and   love - ly   girl,
Se u - na   pu - di - ca   ver - gi - ne

41

Nellie Melba as Violetta, the role she first sang at Covent Garden in 1898. (Covent Garden Archives)

La Traviata

Opera in four parts

Music by Giuseppe Verdi
Libretto by Francesco Maria Piave
(after the play *La dame aux camélias*
by Alexandre Dumas *fils*)
English version by Edmund Tracey

This is the complete Italian libretto by Piave, complete with scene descriptions and stage directions from an early vocal score. These do not necessarily reflect an ENO (or any other modern) production. The original verse lay-out of the libretto has been followed as far as possible. This clearly shows how Piave followed the dialogue of the play and the novel for much of his colloquial and easily-flowing text (many phrases of which are taken directly from the French).

Edmund Tracey's translation was made for performance at the London Coliseum and may also be heard on the EMI recording of that production. It has also been performed in Canada, Australia and South Africa. The passages in square brackets and the stage directions are not part of his translation and are included to give an English version of all the Italian text.

La Traviata was first performed at the Teatro la Fenice, Venice, on March 6, 1853. The first performance in London was at Her Majesty's Theatre on May 24, 1846 (in Italian) and in the USA (New York) on December 3 of the same year.

La Traviata was one of the works in the opening season of opera at Sadler's Wells Theatre, London, in 1931 and was first performed in this translation by Sadler's Wells Opera (now ENO) at the London Coliseum on March 14, 1973.

Violetta Valéry *a demi-mondaine*	soprano
Flora Bervoix *her friend and fellow hostess*	mezzo-soprano
Baron Duphol *Violetta's protector* (Douphol)	baritone
Marquis D'Obigny *friend of Flora* (Il Marchese)	bass
Doctor Grenville (Grenvil)	bass
Gaston *Vicomte de Letorières* (Gastone)	tenor
Alfredo Germont	tenor
Annina *Violetta's maid*	soprano
Joseph *Violetta's servant* (Giuseppe)	tenor
Giorgio Germont *Alfredo's father*	baritone
Servant to Flora	bass
Messenger (Commissario)	bass

Ladies and Gentleman, friends of Violetta and Flora; Servants

The action takes place in and around Paris and the period was specified in early editions of the score and libretto as *circa* 1700. The tradition of mixing the costumes of different periods, with leading ladies often in their own contemporary fashionable clothes, continued into this century.

The first act takes place in August, the second in January and the third in February.

Act One

Prelude. [1,16]
Scene One. *Drawing room in the house of Violetta; doors in centre leading into another room, and at each side. A mantelpiece to the left surmounted by a looking glass; in the centre of the room a table richly spread. Violetta, seated on a sofa, is conversing with her Doctor and several friends, whilst others receive the arriving guests, amongst whom are the Marquis, with Flora on his arm, and the Baron. Introduction* [2]

CHORUS (TENORS)

What a time to arrive at a party!	Dell'invito trascorsa è già l'ora...
What delayed you?	Voi tardaste...

CHORUS (BASSES)

We looked in on Flora.	Giocammo da Flora,
We played cards; no-one noticed the time.	E giocando quell'ore volâr.

VIOLETTA
(going forward to receive them)

Flora, and you, friends, the night lies before us,	Flora, amici, la notte che resta
Laughing, joking, now you make it shine...	D'altre gioie qui fate brillar...
And a glass of champagne is still better...	Fra le tazze è più viva la festa...

FLORA AND MARQUIS

Dare you really enjoy it?	E goder voi potrete?

VIOLETTA

I want to!	Lo voglio;
All these parties and wine are a drug that I need:	Al piacere m'affido, ed io soglio
I try to forget what I feel.	Col tal farmaco i mali sopir.

ALL

Yes, enjoy life and then you'll be well.	Si, la vita s'addoppia al gioir.

Scene Two

GASTON
(entering with Alfredo)

Here's Alfredo Germont, dearest lady;	In Alfredo Germont, o signora,
Another who honours you greatly.	Ecco un altro che molto vi onora;
There is no friend I value so highly.	Pochi amici a lui simili sono.

VIOLETTA
(Violetta gives her hand to Alfredo, who kisses it.)

Then I'm sure I will value him as you do.	Mio Visconte, mercé di tal dono.

(The servants have meanwhile completed preparing the table.)

MARQUIS

Dear Alfredo!	Caro Alfredo...

ALFREDO
(They shake hands.)

My dear Marquis...	Marchese...

GASTON
(to Alfredo)

I told you;	T'ho detto:
Entertainment united with friendship.	L'amistà qui s'intreccia al diletto.

VIOLETTA
(to the servants)

Are you ready?	Pronto è il tutto?

(A servant makes an affirmative sign.)

Come, sit down to supper:	Miei cari, sedete:
All hearts are opened when friends are at ease.	É al convito che s'apre ogni cor.

ALL

With a glass of champagne we forget our troubles.	Ben diceste... le cure segrete
Here we can do as we please.	Fuga sempre l'amico licor.

(All seat themselves; Violetta between Alfredo and Gaston, and Flora between the Baron and the Marquis.)

GASTON
(in an undertone to Violetta)

Young Alfredo adores you.	Sempre Alfredo a voi pensa.

VIOLETTA

You're joking?	Scherzate?

GASTON

Ev'ry day you were ill he was so upset	Egra foste, e ogni dì con affanno
He rushed here for news of...	Qui volò, di voi chiese.

VIOLETTA

You're teasing.	Cessate.
Why should he care for me?	Nulla son io per lui.

GASTON

I'm not lying.	Non v'inganno.

VIOLETTA
(to Alfredo)

Did you really? Tell me why?	Vero è dunque?... onde è ciò?...
I don't follow.	nol comprendo.

ALFREDO
(sighing)

Yes, it is true.	Sì, egli è ver.

VIOLETTA
(to Alfredo)

I am grateful, believe me.	Le mie grazie vi rendo.

(to the Baron)

You, dear Baron, were far less attentive.	Voi, barone, non feste altrettanto...

BARON

After only a few months acquaintance?	Vi conosco da un anno soltanto.

VIOLETTA

But Alfredo has only just met me.	Ed ei solo da qualche minuto.

FLORA
(in an undertone to the Baron)

You would surely do better not to argue.	Meglio fora se aveste taciuto.

BARON
(in an undertone to Flora)

He's an insolent puppy.	M'è increscioso quel giovin...

FLORA

But why?	Perché?
'Au contraire', he's a charming young man.	A me invece simpatico egli è.

GASTON
(to Alfredo)

Are you going to sit silent all evening?	E tu dunque non apri più bocca?

MARQUIS
(to Violetta)

Only our hostess can force him to answer.	È a madama che scuoterlo tocca...

VIOLETTA
(fills Alfredo's glass)

I'll be Hebe and charm you.	Sarò l'Ebe che versa.

ALFREDO
(with gallantry)

May I hope that, Like her, you're immortal.	E ch'io bramo Immortal come quella.

ALL

Violetta! we all drink to you!	Beviamo!

46

To continue the mood of the party, O Barone, né un verso, né un viva
What we need is a toast from the Baron, Troverete in quest'ora giuliva?

(*The Baron makes a gesture of refusal.*)

Or from you! Dunque a te...

(*to Alfredo*)

ALL

Come on, propose a toast! Si, si, un brindisi.

ALFREDO
Will the L'estro
Muse inspire me? Non m'arride...

GASTON
Oh, he's just like a poet! E non se' tu maestro?

ALFREDO
(*to Violetta*)
Would it please you? Vi fia grato?

VIOLETTA
Yes. Si.

ALFREDO
(*rises*)
Yes? I'm inspired. Si... L'ho già in cor.

MARQUIS
Hear the singer! Dunque attenti...

ALL
We attend to his song! Si, attenti al cantor.

Brindisi [3]
ALFREDO

Be happy, and raise your glass with me, Libiamo ne' lieti calici
Here in the palace of beauty; Che la bellezza infiora,
Each hour that passes we feel a duty E la fuggevol ora
To drink and to taste ev'ry joy. S'inebri a voluttà.
We yield to ev'ry ecstasy, Libiam ne—dolci fremiti
For love alone can fire us, Che suscita l'amore.
(*pointing to Violetta*)
Let those bright eyes inspire us. Poiché quell'occhio al core
She rules and we obey. Onnipotente va.
Be happy, and raise your glass with me. Libiamo, amor fra i calici
Kisses and love never cloy. Più caldi baci avrà.

ALL
Ah, be happy and raise your glass. Libiamo, amor fra i calici
Ah, for kisses and love never cloy. Più caldi baci avrà.

VIOLETTA
(*rising*)
With you my dear friends I laughingly Tra voi saprò dividere
Burn up my life in a fever. Il tempo mio giocondo;
Pleasure on pleasure is all I crave for, Tutto è follia nel mondo
No time for tears or sighs. Ciò che non è piacer.
Enjoy the moment recklessly, Godiam, fugace e rapido
For love has no true power. È il gaudio dell'amore;
It blossoms like a flower, È un fior che nasce e muore,
Then withers, fades and dies. Né più si può goder.
Enjoy life in fev'rish ecstasy. Godiam... c'invita un fervido
What else can we prize? Accento lusinghier.

ALL
Ah, we taste all the joys of night Godiam... la tazza e il cantico
In our drinking and singing and laughter. La notte abbella e il riso;
The dawn of the morning after In questo paradiso
Will find us in heaven here. Ne scopra il nuovo dì.

VIOLETTA
(*to Alfredo*)
The point of life is excitement. La vita è nel tripudio.

47

For one who has no true lover.

ALFREDO
(*to Violetta*)
Quando non s'ami ancora.

VIOLETTA
(*to Alfredo*)
Too late for me to discover.

Nol dite a chi l'ignora.

ALFREDO
(*to Violetta*)
My destiny is clear.

È il mio destin così...

ALL

Ah, we taste all the joys of the night
In our drinking and singing and laughter.
The dawn of the morning after
Will find us in heaven here.

Godiam... la tazza e il cantico
La notte abbella e il riso;
In questo paradiso
Ne scopra il nuovo dì.

Music is heard in the further room. [4] *Waltz and Duet*

What's that?

Che è ciò?

VIOLETTA

There is the music, shall we have dancing?

Non gradireste ora le danze?

ALL

What a good idea! We will enjoy a dance.

Oh, il gentil pensier!... tutti accettiamo.

VIOLETTA

Let us go in then...

Usciamo dunque...

(*They approach the centre door when Violetta suddenly falters.*)

Oh...

Ohimè...

ALL

What is it?

Che avete?...

VIOLETTA

Nothing,

Nulla,

Nothing.

Nulla.

ALL

What is the matter?

Che mai v'arresta?...

VIOLETTA
(*She attempts to walk a few steps.*)

I'm better...

Usciamo...

(*She is forced to stop and take a seat.*)

Oh Heaven!

Oh Dio!...

ALL

Violetta!

Ancora!...

ALFREDO

Let me help you.

Voi soffrite?

ALL

What is the matter?

O ciel!... c'è questo?

VIOLETTA

I thought that I was fainting!
Please start the dancing...

Un tremito che provo... Or là passate...

(*Points to the inner apartment.*)

I will be there very soon.

Tra poco anch'io sarò...

ALL

Rest for a moment.

Come bramate.

All go into the further room except Alfredo. **Scene Three.** *Violetta rises and looks at herself in the glass.*

VIOLETTA

I look so pale!

Oh qual pallor!...

(*turns, and sees Alfredo*)

It's you!

Voi qui!...

ALFREDO

I came to see if

Cessata è l'ansia

You were all right.

Che vi turbò?

48

VIOLETTA

I'm better.   Sto meglio.

ALFREDO

You must be careful,   Ah, in cotal guisa
You are so fragile. Take care I beg you.   V'ucciderete... aver v'è d'uopo cura
This sort of life will kill you.   Dell'esser vostro...

VIOLETTA

I know no other.   E lo potrei?

ALFREDO

If you   Se mia
Could love me, how closely I would   Foste, custode io veglierei pe' vostri
guard you and keep you
Safe from harm.   Soavi dì.

VIOLETTA

You'd guard me? I know of no-one   Che dite?... ha forse alcuno
Who would do that.   Cura di me?

ALFREDO
(ardently)

Only because you have no   Perché nessuno al mondo
Lover.   V'ama...

VIOLETTA

Not one?   Nessun?

ALFREDO

Only Alfredo.   Tranne sol io.

VIOLETTA
(laughing)

Alfredo?   Gli è vero!...
Now you remind me of your secret passion.   Sì grande amor dimenticato avea...

ALFREDO

You're laughing! Your heart is beating?   Ridete?...e in voi v'ha un core?...

VIOLETTA

My heart... Yes, beating... but why,   Un cor?... sì...forse e a che
why do you ask me?   lo richiedete?

ALFREDO

It can't be beating... or you'd   Ah, se ciò fosse, non potreste
never make fun   allora
Of love.   Celiar.

VIOLETTA

Are you in earnest?   Dite davvero?...

ALFREDO

I don't deceive you.   Io non v'inganno.

VIOLETTA

And so, how long have you loved me?   Da molto è che mi amate?

ALFREDO

For just a year now.   Ah, sì, da un anno.
I saw a vision ethereal   [5]   Un dì, felice, eterea,
Glittering there before me,   Mi balenaste innante,
And from that day of glory   E da quel dì tremante
I was in love from afar.   Vissi d'ignoto amor.
Ah, it is love and love is our destiny. [6] Di quell'amor ch'è palpito.
Love universal, the love that brings us   Dell' universo intero,
    together.
Mystery rules us, mystery rules for ever: Misterioso, altero,
Cruel and blissful beat of the heart!   Croce e delizia al cor.

VIOLETTA

This is all far too serious...   [7]   Ah, se ciò è ver, fuggitemi...
Friendship is all I offer.   Solo amistade io v'offro:
The destiny you proffer   Amar non so, né soffro
Is greater than I aspire to.   Un così eroico amor.
I must be frank and say to you: Io sono franca, ingenua;
I am a simple woman: Altra cercar dovete;

49

So try to forget me and find Another for your love.	Non arduo troverete Dimenticarmi allor.

GASTON
(at the door)

Ha, ha! What are you doing?	Ebben? ... che diavol fate?

VIOLETTA

Just talking nonsense ...	Si folleggiava ...

GASTON

Just as you please. I'll leave you ...	Ah! ah! ... sta ben ... restate.

(He leaves them.)

VIOLETTA
(to Alfredo)

And so we are agreed ... Love is forbidden?	Amor dunque non più ... Vi garba il patto?

ALFREDO

I shall obey you.	Io v'obbedisco ...

(going)

I'll leave you.	Parto ...

VIOLETTA

You're really going?	A tal giungeste?

(takes a flower from her breast)

Then take one of these flowers.	Prendete questo fiore.

ALFREDO

But why?	Perché?

VIOLETTA

You could return it.	Per riportarlo ...

ALFREDO
(returning)

May I?	Quando?

VIOLETTA

When It is nearly faded.	Quando Sarà appassito.

ALFREDO

You mean ... tomorrow.	Oh ciel! domani ...

VIOLETTA

I mean ... Tomorrow.	Ebbene, Domani.

ALFREDO
(takes the flower with rapture)

I've never been so happy!	Io son felice!

VIOLETTA

You say you really love me?	D'amarmi dite ancora?

ALFREDO
(going)

Ah, I love you with all my heart.	Oh, quanto v'amo! ...

VIOLETTA

You're leaving.	Partite?

ALFREDO
(returns and kisses her hand)

Thank you!	Parto.

VIOLETTA

Tomorrow.	Addio.

ALFREDO

I am so happy.	Di più non bramo.

Exit Alfredo. **Scene Four.** *The others return; all are heated with dancing.* Stretta [8]

ALL

We present ourselves before you; What a splendid night of feasting. Dearest lady we adore you, But the dawn is in the east. Paris is a round of pleasure And the season's just begun;	Si ridesta in ciel l'aurora, E n'è forza di partir; Mercé a voi, gentil signora, Di sì splendido gioir. La città di feste è piena, Volge il tempo dei piacer;

50

We must sleep and take our leisure,
So that we enjoy the fun.

Exeunt. **Scene Five.** *Recitative and Aria*

Nel riposo ancor la lena
Si ritempri per goder.

VIOLETTA

I wonder! I wonder! I'll never
Forget the things he told me!
But would it be unlucky to love
  sincerely?
Ah, my spirit is full of doubt and
  anguish!
No man has ever made me love him!

Oh joy I never knew of, to be in
  love and be loved!
Dare I spurn what he offers
To choose these empty follies and
  waste my life?
Is he the one I dream about?   [9]
Hiding my tears in laughter,
I have so often pictured him
Ev'rything I have longed for.
Fancy his simple constancy
When I was sick with fever!
I feel a strange new shiver—
Can it be I'm in love?
Ah, it is love and love is our destiny:
Love universal, this love that brings us
  together!
Mystery rules us for ever:
Cruel and blissful beat of the heart!
[To me, when still a girl,
a pure and timid desire
sweetly marked this man
as lord of my life;
when, in the heavens
I would see his beauty's ray,
my whole being fed upon
that divine illusion.]

È strano! ... è strano! ... in core
Scolpiti ho quegli accenti!
Saria per me sventura in serio
  amore?
Che risolvi, o turbata anima mia?

Null'uomo ancora t'accendeva ...
  O gioia
Ch'io non conobbi, essere amata
  amando! ...
E sdegnarla poss'io
Per l'aride follie del viver mio?

    Ah, fors'è lui che l'anima
Solinga ne' tumulti
Godea sovente pingere
De' suoi colori occulti! ...
Lui che modesto e vigile
All'egre soglie ascese,
E nuova fabbre accese,
Destandomi all'amor,
A quell'amor ch'è palpito
Dell'universo intero,
Misterioso, altero,
Croce e delizia al cor.
    A me fanciulla, un candido
E trepido desire
Quest'effigiò dolcissimo
Signor dell'avvenire,
Quando ne'ciel il raggio
Di sua beltà vedea,
E tutta me pascea
Di quel divino error.
Sentia che amore è palpito
Dell'universo intero,
Misterioso, altero,
Croce e delizia al cor!

(She stands pensively then rouses herself.)

It can't be! It can't be! These dreams
  are hopeless nonsense.
Wretched Violetta! Lonely,
Entirely friendless, with no-one
To protect me in this crowded
Desert they call Paris!
What must I do? What can I hope for?
Enjoy life and drown myself in ev'ry
  wild excess.
Give me freedom to be happy,   [10]
All my life enjoying, enjoying:
Let me drink at ev'ry party,
Let me dance at ev'ry ball!
Never weeping and never sighing,
Always singing, always laughing!
Oh I'm only just beginning
New excitements: I'll try them all.

Follie! ... follie! ... delirio vano è
  questo! ...
Povera donna, sola,
Abbandonata in questo
Popoloso deserto
Che appellano Parigi,
Che spero or più? ... Che far degg'io? ...
  Gioire,
Di voluttà nei vortici perire.
    Sempre libera degg'io
Folleggiar di gioia in gioia,
Vo' che scorra il viver mio
Pei sentieri del piacer.
Nasca il giorno, o il giorno muoia,
Sempre lieta ne' ritrovi
A diletti sempre nuovi
Dee volare il mio pensier.

ALFREDO
(under the balcony)

Ah, Love is our destiny: [6]
Love universal, the love that
  brings us together!

Di quell'amor ch'è palpito:
etc.

51

Alfredo!

Mystery rules us for ever.
Cruel and blissful beat of the heart!

It can't be! It can't be! Ah no!
Give me freedom to be happy! *etc.*

VIOLETTA
Alfredo!

ALFREDO
Misterioso, altero
Croce e delizia al cor.

VIOLETTA
Follie!... follie!... delirio vano è questo!...
Sempre libera deggi'io. *etc.*

Curtain.

Francesco Maria Piave, the librettist. (Archivio Storico Ricordi)

Act Two

Scene One. *A room on the ground floor of a country house near Paris. In the centre, at the back, a mantelpiece with clock, mirror etc.. A glass door on each side shows the garden; other doors lead within the house. Chairs, books, a writing table, etc.. Enter Alfredo in hunting costume. Recitative and Aria*

ALFREDO
(putting away his gun)

I'm never happy if she is not beside me.	Lunge da lei per me non v'ha diletto!
Three months ago Violetta	Volaron già tre lune
For my sake fled from Paris:	Dacché la mia Violetta
She left it all behind, her riches, her lovers,	Agli per me lasciò, dovizie, onori,
And all the brilliant parties	E le pompose feste
Where she had always conquered	Ove, agli omaggi avvezza,
The heart of ev'ry man with all her beauty.	Vedea schiavo ciascun di sua bellezza ...
And now contented in quiet country pastimes,	Ed or contenta in questi ameni luoghi
She lives only for me. Here by her side	Tutto scorda per me. Qui presso a lei
I renew my ambitions:	Io rinascer mi sento,
All my dreams of a true and lasting passion,	E dal soffio d'amor rigenerato
And in its tender joys past grief is forgotten.	Scordo ne' gaudi suoi tutto il passato.
My life was too impetuous, [11]	De' miei bollenti spiriti
Thoughtless, entirely selfish.	Il giovanile ardore
She taught me how to realise	Ella temprò col placido
The sweet and tender love of the heart!	Sorriso dell'amore!
One day she whisper'd: "Live with me!	Dal dì che disse: vivere
I love you, I am your faithful love!"	Io voglio a te fedel,
That is my only memory,	Dell'universo immemore
I live in Heav'n above.	Io vivo quasi in ciel.

Scene Two. *Enter Annina, in travelling clothes.*

ALFREDO

Annina, where have you been?	Annina, donde vieni?

ANNINA

Up to Paris.	Da Parigi.

ALFREDO

Some special reason?	Chi tel commise?

ANNINA

Yes, my mistress sent me.	Fu la mia signora.

ALFREDO

But why?	Perché?

ANNINA

To sell her horses and her carriage,	Per alienar cavalli, cocchi,
All her furs and diamonds.	E quanto ancor possiede.

ALFREDO

Are you serious?	Che mai sento!

ANNINA

The life you're leading has cost a lot of money ...	Lo spendio è grande a viver qui solinghi ...

ALFREDO

Why not tell me?	E tacevi?

ANNINA

I had to promise silence.	Mi fu il silenzio imposto.

ALFREDO

To promise! What sum is needed?	Imposto! ... or v'abbisogna? ...

ANNINA

One thousand louis.	Mille luigi.

ALFREDO

I'll pay it ... I'll go to Paris ...	Or vanne ... andrò a Parigi.
And yet your mistress must never know you told me.	Questo colloquio ignori la signora.
I still have time to put it all in order. Go! Go!	Il tutto valgo a riparare ancora.

53

Exit Annina. **Scene Three.**

ALFREDO

I hate myself, I'm so ashamed!	O mio rimorso! O infamia!
How could I be so selfish!	Io vissi in tale errore!
But now at last I know the truth,	Ma il turpe sonno a frangere
I'll make amends today!	Il ver mi balenò.
Be still a while and wait, my heart,	Per poco in seno acquetati,
I swear I shall restore your honour,	O grido dell'onore;
I give my word to make amends	M'avrai securo vindice;
And wash my shame away.	Quest'onta laverò.

Exit. **Scene Four.** *Enter Violetta with papers. Recitative and Duet*

VIOLETTA

Alfredo? Alfredo?

ANNINA

He has just set out for Paris. Per Parigi or or partiva.

VIOLETTA

To stay for long? E tornerà?

ANNINA

No, only till this evening ... Pria che tramonti il giorno ...
I said I'd tell you. Dirvel m'impose ...

VIOLETTA

How curious! È strano!

JOSEPH
(enters and presents a letter to Violetta)

For you. Per voi ...

VIOLETTA
(She takes it.)

Thank you. A gentleman Sta bene. In breve
Is calling here on business. You may admit Giungerà un uom d'affari ... entri
him. all'istante.

Exeunt Annina and Joseph. **Scene Five.**

VIOLETTA
(opens the letter)

Ha, ha! Our clever Flora knows Ah, ah scopriva Flora il mio
my secret: ritiro! ...
We are asked to a party there this evening! E m'invita a danzar per questa sera!
(throws the letter on a table)
It's like another world ... Invan m'aspetterà ...

JOSEPH

A gentleman is here ma'am! È qui un signore ...

VIOLETTA

It will be my lawyer. Ah! sarà lui che attendo.

(signalling to Joseph to admit him)

GERMONT

You're Violetta Valéry? Madamigella Valéry?

VIOLETTA

I am, sir. Son io.

GERMONT

I am the father of Alfredo. D'Alfredo il padre in me vedete!

VIOLETTA
(surprised, motions him to be seated)
You? Voi!

GERMONT
(seating himself)

Yes, of that madman. How did you Si, dell'incauto, che a ruina
bewitch him? corre,
Why choose my son to ruin? Ammaliato da voi.

VIOLETTA
(rising, with resentment)

Sir, you address a woman, and this is Donna son io, signore, ed in mia casa;
my house.

54

I'm afraid I must leave you,   Ch'io vi lasci assentite,
More for your sake than mine.   Più per voi che per me.

(going)

GERMONT

(How gracious!) Wait though ...   (Quai modi!) Pure ...

VIOLETTA

Someone has misinformed you.   Tratto in error voi foste.

(returns and seats herself)

GERMONT

He is planning to   De' suoi beni
Give you his fortune.   Dono vuol farvi ...

VIOLETTA

He would never dare to ...   Non l'osò finora ...
I would refuse.   Rifiuterei.

GERMONT

(looking round)

You live in style here.   Pur tanto lusso ...

VIOLETTA

(gives him a paper)

This contract   A tutti
Has so far been secret... but you may see it ...   È mistero quest'atto... A voi nol sia.

GERMONT

(reads the paper)

Heav'ns! What does this mean? You are   Ciel! che discopro! D'ogni vostro avere
really selling
All your worldly possessions?   Or volete spogliarvi?
What a pity your past must always shame   Ah, il passato perché, perché v'accusa?
you!

VIOLETTA

(with ardour)

My past is over... I love Alfredo   Più non esiste... or amo Alfredo,
and God   e Dio
Has heard my prayer and granted me   Lo cancellò col pentimento mio.
his pardon!

GERMONT

Noble and gen'rous feelings.   Nobili sensi invero!

VIOLETTA

How reassuring   Oh, come dolce
To hear you speak so kindly!   Mi suona il vostro accento!

GERMONT

(rising)

Now I can ask you   Ed a tai sensi
To sacrifice those feelings.   Un sacrificio chieggo...

VIOLETTA

(rising)

Ah, no, you must not.   Ah no, tacete...
You want to ask for something that would   Terribil cosa chiedereste certo...
hurt me.
I foresaw it, I knew it... Ah, I was far too   Il previdi... v'attesi... era felice
Happy.   Troppo...

GERMONT

Alfredo's father   D'Alfredo il padre
Implores you to have pity on the fate   La sorte, l'avvenir domanda or qui
Of both his children.   De' suoi due figli.

VIOLETTA

Both your children?   Di due figli?

GERMONT

Yes.   Sì.
I have a daughter sent from God,   [12]   Pura siccome un angelo
Innocent and appealing;   Iddio mi die' una figlia;
Alfredo now disowns us both   Se Alfredo nega riedere
And scorns all family feeling.   In seno alla famiglia,
She has a lover young and true,   L'amato e amante giovane,

They are engaged to marry;
Now he will have to break the tie
That made them both so fond and
happy.
Ah, do not turn to bitter thorns
Roses so sweet and fair!
Ah, do not turn to bitter thorns
The roses of their love!
Ah, don't deny your sympathy;
No, no, you cannot close your heart
to me!

Cui sposa andar dovea,
Or si ricusa al vincolo
Che lieti ne rendea...
Deh, non mutate in triboli
Le rose dell'amor.
Ai preghi miei resistere
Non voglia il vostro cor.
(*repeat*)

VIOLETTA

Ah, I follow! I ought to spend a short
while
Away from my Alfredo! I will suffer,
Suffer so much... Still...

Ah, comprendo... dovrò per alcun tempo

Da Alfredo allontanarmi... doloroso
Fora per me... pur...

GERMONT

That's not what I'm asking.

Non è ciò che chiedo.

VIOLETTA

Heaven! There's something further?
I've tried to help you!

Cielo, che più cercate?... offersi assai!

GERMONT

Try still harder!

Pur non basta...

VIOLETTA

You're asking me to give
Him up for ever?

Volete che per sempre
A lui rinunzi?

GERMONT

It must be.

È d'uopo!...

VIOLETTA

Ah no! Never!

Ah, no... giammai!

Do you realise I adore him,
And I live my whole life for him?
There is no-one, friend or family,
None to guide me or to help me;
And Alfredo has given me
His word to live for me.
Do you realise I am dying?
Yes, I swear it, I am dying.
And too little time is remaining
For me now to leave Alfredo!
Such a torment would be horrible
And I could never bear it.
I would prefer to die.

[13]   Non sapete quale affetto
Vivo, immenso m'arda in petto?
Che né amici, né parenti
Io non conto tra i viventi?
E che Alfredo m'ha giurato
Che in lui tutto io troverò?
Non sapete che colpita
D'atro morbo è la mia vita?
Che già presso il fin ne vedo?
Ch'io mi separi da Alfredo?
Ah, il supplizio è si spietato,
(*repeat*)
Che morir preferirò.

GERMONT

The sacrifice is bitter,
But hear me out, I beg of you.
You are so lovely and still so young...
Some other...

È grave il sacrifizio,
Ma pur tranquilla udite...
Bella voi siete e giovane...
Col tempo...

VIOLETTA

Ah no, don't say it...
You mean well... but I cannot change:
I never could love another.

Ah, più non dite...
V'intendo... m'è impossibile...
Lui solo amar vogl'io.

GERMONT

You think so, yet you know
How fickle men can be.

Sia pure... ma volubile
Sovente è l'uom...

VIOLETTA
(*overcome*)

Oh heaven!

Gran Dio!

GERMONT

A day will come when making love
No longer will excite you:
An empty stale monotony is all
That can unite you...
For you no future happiness of

Un dì, quando le veneri
Il tempo avrà fugate,
Fia presto il tedio a sorgere...
Che sarà allor?... pensate...
Per voi non avran balsamo

Sweet and true affection,
For this affair will never gain
The grace of heaven.

I più soavi affeti!
Poiché dal ciel non furono
Tai nodi benedetti.

VIOLETTA
I know it!　　　　　　　　　　　　　È vero!

GERMONT
　　　Ah, do not now deceive yourself　　　　Ah, dunque sperdasi
By trusting in delusion:　　　　　　　　Tal sogno seduttore...
Say you will be, for my sake,　　　　　　Siate di mia famiglia
An angel of consolation ...　　　　　　L'angiol consolatore...
Violetta, won't you pity me?　　　　　　Violetta, deh, pensateci
We still may be in time ...　　　　　　Ne siete in tempo ancor,
The voice of God inspires me,　　　　　È Dio che ispira, o giovine,
His voice inspires a father's words.　　　Tai detti a un genitor.

VIOLETTA
(in an agony of grief)

So I have sinned and my life is committed:　(Così alla misera—ch'è un dì caduta,
No hope of pardon for me is permitted.　　Di più risorgere—speranza è muta!
God may be merciful, He may forgive me;　Se pur benefico—le indulga Iddio,
Man has no pity, he has no heart.　　　　L'uomo implacabile—per lei serà.)
Man is implacable, he has no heart.　　　*(repeat)*

(weeping)
Ah! Comfort your gentle girl　　　　[14] Dite alla giovine—si bella e
　so pure and lovely,　　　　　　　　pura
Tell how a victim once suffered　　　Ch'avvi una vittima—della
　so lonely:　　　　　　　　　　　sventura,
She who had a single ray of　　　　Cui resta un unico—raggio di
　happiness,　　　　　　　　　　bene...
She shut it out of her life and　　　Che a lei il sacrifica—e che
　she died.　　　　　　　　　　morrà!

GERMONT
Anguish breaks your heart, poor　　Si, piangi, o misera...—supremo,
　Violetta.　　　　　　　　　　　il veggo,
I am demanding so great a sacrifice,　È il sacrificio—ch'ora ti chieggo.
Asking you now to give up Alfredo,
I feel your suffering deep in your spirit.　Sento nell'anima—già le tue pene;
You must have courage and your noble　Coraggio... e il nobile—cor vincerà.
　nature will win in the end.

(pause)
VIOLETTA
Now command me!　　　　　　　Or imponete.

GERMONT
　　Tell him you don't love him.　　　　　　Non amarlo ditegli.

VIOLETTA
He won't believe me.　　　　　　Nol crederà.

GERMONT
　　Then leave him.　　　　　　　Partite.

VIOLETTA
　　He will follow.　　　　　　　　　　Seguirammi.

GERMONT
Well then...　　　　　　　　Allor...

VIOLETTA
　Embrace me as your daughter... Then I'll　Qual figlia m'abbracciate...forte
Have strength again.　　　　　　Così sarò.

(They embrace.)
　　I'll give you back Alfredo,　　　　　Tra breve ei vi fia reso,
But he'll be broken-hearted. He'll　Ma afflitto oltre ogni dire. A
　need your comfort...　　　　　　suo conforto
Be ready to console him.　　　　Di colà volerete.

(She indicates that he should wait in the garden as she prepares to write.)
GERMONT
　　What to tell him?　　　　　　　　　Che pensate?

VIOLETTA

I fear that if I told you, you might oppose it.	Sapendol, v'opporreste al pensier mio.

GERMONT

How unselfish! How can I repay your noble goodness?	Generosa!... e per voi che far poss'io?

VIOLETTA
(*turning to him*)

I'll die, but you must promise me	Morrò!... la mia memoria
You won't ever let him curse me;	Non fia ch'ei maledica,
You'll tell him of my sacrifice	Se le mie pene orribili
And how you had to force me!	Vi sia chi almen gli dica.
Now promise me that one day	Conosca il sacrifizio
You'll tell him all that happened...	Ch'io consumai d'amor...
I will be true until the end.	Che sarà suo fin l'ultimo
I'm his until I die.	Sospiro del mio cor.

GERMONT

No, gen'rous girl, you shall not die:	No generosa, vivere,
A sweet path lies before you.	E lieta, voi dovrete,
Your tears shall be rewarded	Mercé di queste lagrime
And the angels will smile upon you!	Dal cielo un giorno avrete;
Your tears will be rewarded,	Premiato il sacrifizio
Yes, all that you have suffered,	Sarà del vostro amor;
And you'll be proud, you noble girl	D'un'opra così nobile
Of all that you have done.	Sarete fiera allor.

VIOLETTA

There's someone here. Please leave me.	Qui giunge alcun! partite!...

GERMONT

With all my heart I thank you...	Ah, grato v'è il cor mio!...

VIOLETTA

Ah, leave me.	[Partite.]
This may be our last meeting...	Non ci vedrem più forse...

GERMONT AND VIOLETTA
(*They embrace.*)

May you be happy. God bless you!	Siate felice... addio!...

Exit Germont through the garden door. **Scene Six.** *Recitative.*

VIOLETTA

God give me strength to bear it!	Dammi tu forza, o cielo!

(*She rings the bell then seats herself and writes.*)

ANNINA

You rang for me, ma'am?	Mi richiedeste?

VIOLETTA

Yes, go straight to Paris		Sì, reca tu stessa
With this letter.	Questo foglio...	

ANNINA
(*sees the address, surprised*)

Oh!	Oh!

VIOLETTA

Be quiet... Do not argue.	Silenzio... va all'istante.

(*Exit Annina.*)

Now I must tell Alfredo...	Ed or si scriva a lui...

(*She seats herself again to write.*)

What shall I say? Ah, who will give me courage?	[15] Che gli dirò? Chi men darà il coraggio?

(*She writes and seals the letter. Enter Alfredo.*)

ALFREDO

What's that?	Che fai?

VIOLETTA
(*hiding her letter*)

Nothing.	Nulla.

ALFREDO

You're writing?   Scrivevi?

VIOLETTA
(*with embarrassment*)
Yes... No...   Sì... no...

ALFREDO
You're pale and trembling! You wrote a   Qual turbamento!... a chi scrivevi?
letter?

VIOLETTA
To you.   A te...

ALFREDO
Show me the letter.   Dammi quel foglio.

VIOLETTA
Read it later.   No, per ora...

ALFREDO
Ah, forgive me... I'm feeling rather nervous.   Mi perdona... son io preoccupato.

VIOLETTA
(*rising*)
Ah, why?   Che fu?

ALFREDO
Well, it's my father...   Giunse mio padre...

VIOLETTA
Have you seen him?   Lo vedesti?

ALFREDO
Ah no, he called and left this angry letter.   Ah no; severo scritto mi lasciava...
I still expect him. When he sees you he'll   Però l'attendo, t'amerà in vederti.
love you.

VIOLETTA
(*with agitation*)
You mustn't let him see me.   Ch'ei qui non mi sorprenda...
It's best if you're alone here...   Lascia che m'allontani... tu
Try to calm him... Then I will beg him   lo calma...
to be kind.
(*scarcely suppressing her tears*)
He will not try to make us part...   Ai piedi suoi mi getterò... divisi
We will be happy because you love me,   Ei più non ne vorrà... sarem felici...
Alfredo you love me... won't you say it?   Perché tu m'ami, Alfredo, non è vero?

ALFREDO
I love you! Why this crying?   Oh, quanto... Perché piangi?

VIOLETTA
I had to cry. I couldn't help it.   Di lagrime avea d'uopo... or son
But now I'm calmer... Alfredo, see   tranquilla...
  I'm smiling...   Lo vedi?... ti sorrido...
(*making an effort*)
I'll be there, just outside,   Sarò là, tra quei fior presso a
Yes, I'll be near you, in the   te sempre.
garden, always near.
Love me Alfredo, love me as much   [16]   Amami Alfredo, quant'io t'amo...
as I love you... And now farewell!   Addio.

Exit hastily into the garden. **Scene Seven.** *Recitative and Aria.*

ALFREDO
That heart is mine, forever, and how I love   Ah, vive sol quel core all'amor mio!...
her!
(*He seats himself, opens a book and looks at the clock.*)
It's very unlike my father   È tardi: ed oggi forse
To visit me at this hour.   Più non verrà mio padre.

JOSEPH
(*entering hastily*)
My young mistress has left us...   La signora è partita...
In a coach that was waiting;   L'attendeva un calesse, e sulla via
I saw them go at a gallop off to
  Paris... Annina too: Già corre di Parigi... Annina pure
She set out before my mistress.   Prima di lei spariva.

59

ALFREDO

I know, don't worry.   Il so, ti calma.

JOSEPH

(What can it mean?)   (Che vuol dir ciò?)

(Exit.)

ALFREDO

Perhaps she's gone   Va forse d'ogni avere
To hasten the sale of all her property...   Ad affrettar la perdita... Ma Annina
Annina will get there first.   Lo impedirà.

(Germont is seen at a distance, crossing the garden.)

There's someone in the garden.   Qualcuno è nel giardino!
Who's there?   Chi è la?...

(about to go out)

A GARDENER

(at the door)

You're monsieur Germont?   Il signor Germont?

ALFREDO

I am, yes.   Son io.

GARDENER

Here's a note from a lady for you...   Una dama
I said I'd bring it.   Da un cocchio, per voi, di qua non lunge,
Her coach drove off for Paris.   Mi diede questo scritto...

He gives a letter to Alfredo, receives money from him and leaves. **Scene Eight.**

ALFREDO

From Violetta! But why am I so nervous?   Di Violetta! Perché son io commosso!...
Is she writing to ask me to join her?   A raggiungerla forse ella m'invita...
I'm trembling!... Oh God!... Have courage!   Io tremo!... Oh ciel!... Coraggio!...

(opens the letter)

"Alfredo, as soon as you have read   "Alfredo, al giungervi di questo foglio..."
    this letter..."

(exclaiming)

Ah!   Ah!

(turning to find himself in the arms of his father)

Dearest father!   Padre mio!...

GERMONT

Alfredo!...   Mio figlio!...

I know you're suff'ring... Come, no   Oh, quanto soffri!... tergi, ah,
   more sorrow...   tergi il pianto...
Return and cheer your father,   Ritorna di tuo padre orgoglio e
   beloved Alfredo!   vanto.

(Alfredo sits down by the table in despair, his face buried in his hands.)

GERMONT

In Provence, your native land   Di Provenza il mar, il suol—
   we all long for your return,   chi dal cor ti cancellò?
Who has stolen you away   Al natio fulgente sol—
   from our blue and sunny skies?   qual destino ti furò?
Oh how happy you once were—   Oh, rammenta pur nel duol—
   not a trace of grief or pain.   ch'ivi gioia a te brillò;
You must know that only there   E che pace colà sol— su te
   peace will shine on you again...   splendere ancor può.
God hear my prayer!   Dio mi guidò!
How we missed you, dearest boy,   Ah! il tuo vecchio genitor—
   you will never, never know;   tu non sai quanto soffri...
How we hung our heads in shame   Te lontano, di squallor—
   when you left without a word!   il suo tetto si coprì...
But I've found you once again   Ma se alfin ti trovo ancor,—
   and I will not let you go,   se in me speme non fallì,
If your honour still can claim   Se la voce dell'onor—
   to instruct you what to do.   in te appien non ammutì,
God led me here to bring you home.   Dio m'esaudì!

(He embraces Alfredo.)

Won't you answer your father, Alfredo?   Né rispondi d'un padre all'affetto?

ALFREDO

I'm tormented by jealousy and fury.   Mille serpi divoranmi il petto...
(repulsing his father)
Father leave me!   Mi lasciate.

GERMONT

          Alfredo!   Lasciarti!

ALFREDO
(resolved)
    (I'll have vengeance!)   (Oh vendetta!)

GERMONT

We'll be starting, Alfredo... now hurry.   Non più indugi; partiamo... t'affretta...

ALFREDO

It was the Baron!   (Ah, fu Douphol!)

GERMONT

    So, shall we go?   M'ascolti tu?

ALFREDO

     No!   No.

GERMONT

All my love and my pleading in vain?	Dunque invano trovato t'avrò!
No, no, I cannot preach at you;	No, non udrai rimproveri;
We'll bury what has happened;	Copriam d'oblio il passato;
My love for you has guided me	L'amor che m'ha guidato,
And I can understand.	Sa tutto perdonar.
Come home and greet your family,	Vieni, i tuoi cari in giubilo
Embrace your loving sister;	Con me rivedi ancora:
To know that you have missed her	A chi penò finora
Will fill her heart with joy.	Tal gioia non negar.
A father and a sister implore your	Un padre ed una suora
consolation, dearest boy.	T'affretta a consolar.

ALFREDO
(rousing himself, sees Flora's letter on the table, reads it again, and exclaims)

Ah! She's gone to Flora's!	Ah!... ell'è alla festa! volisi
I will go and I will take my revenge.	L'offesa a vendicar.

(He rushes off distractedly, followed by Germont.)

GERMONT

Come back here, Alfredo!   Che dici? Ah, ferma!

Curtain.

*

Scene Nine. *A richly furnished apartment in Flora's mansion. Doors at both sides and in the centre. A gaming table to the right. A table with refreshments to the left. Sofas, etc.. Flora, the Marquis, Doctor and other guests enter from the left in conversation. Finale Two* [18]

FLORA

The surprise is a band of dancing gipsies,	Avrem, lieta di maschere la notte:
With Gaston as their leader.	N'è duce il viscontino...
Will Violetta and Alfredo join us tonight?	Violetta e Alfredo anco invitai.

MARQUIS

Surely you've heard the story?	La novità ignorate?
Violetta will come here with the Baron.	Violetta e Germont sono disguinti.

THE DOCTOR AND FLORA

Not really!   Fia vero?...

MARQUIS

    She has left Alfredo for ever.   Ella verrà qui col barone.

DOCTOR

I saw them yesterday, they both seemed so   Li vidi ieri ancor... parean felici.
   happy.

(A noise is heard offstage.)

But listen, you hear them?   Silenzio... udite?...

(They advance towards the right.)

ALL
       All our friends are ready!   Giungono gli amici.

Scene Ten. *Ladies disguised as gypsies enter. Chorus of Gipsies* [10]

GIPSIES

We're gipsy fortune tellers:	Noi siamo zingarelle
Permit us to salute you.	Venute da lontano;
We see into the future,	D'ognuno sulla mano
We read it in your hand.	Leggiamo l'avvenir.
When we consult the stars	Se consultiam le stelle
They tell us what we want to know,	Null'avvi a noi d'oscuro,
No mystery too dark for us	E i casi del futuro
To shed a ray of light!	Possiamo altrui predir.
We make the future bright	
And we make you understand.	
Watch closely! Fairest lady,	Vediamo! Voi, signora.

(scanning Flora's hand)
You must beware of rivals.   Rivali alquante avete.
(reading the hand of the Marquis)
This nobleman betrays you,   Marchese, voi non siete
He has a roving eye.   Model di fedeltà.

FLORA
(to the Marquis)
So you have been unfaithful?   Fate il galante ancora?
I'll pay you out, I promise.   Ben, vo'me la paghiate...

MARQUIS
(to Flora)
You don't believe this rubbish?   Che dianci vi pensate?...
It's all a pack of lies.   L'accusa è falsità.

FLORA
A snake will shed his colour,   La volpe lascia il pelo,
But not his evil nature,   Non abbandona il vizio...
So you, my dear, be grateful   Marchese mio, giudizio...
I don't scratch out your eyes.   O vi farò pentir.

ALL
Enough, let's draw a cover   Su via, si stenda un velo
On jealousy and sorrow.   Sui fatti del passato;
What matters is tomorrow,   Già quel ch'è stato è stato,
The past is dead and gone.   Badiamo (Badate) all'avvenir.

The Marquis presses Flora's hand. **Scene Eleven.** *Gaston and others, disguised as Spanish Matadors and Picadors, rush in from the right. Chorus of Spanish Matadors*

GASTON WITH MATADORS

We are heroes, in Spain they adore us;	Di Madride noi siam mattadori,
In the bullring we all are victorious.	Siamo i prodi del circo de'tori,
We are here to enjoy life in Paris,	Testé giunti a godere del chiasso
We are ready for wine and for feasting.	Che a Parigi si fa pel bue grasso;
Shall we tell you a wonderful story,	E una storia, se udire vorrete,
Full of passionate love and of glory?	Quali amanti noi siamo saprete.

THE OTHERS
Bravo, bravo, come tell us a story,   Sì, sì, bravi; narrate, narrate:
Full of passion and glory.   Con piacere l'udremo...

GASTON WITH MATADORS
                    Listen closely.   Ascoltate.

Here's Piquillo, strong and handsome,	[20]	È Piquillo un bel gagliardo
Biscay's leading matador.		Biscaglino mattador:
By his skill he won a King's ransom,		Forte il braccio, fiero il guardo,
In the ring so brave and sure.		Delle giostre egli è signor.
Then he lost his heart completely;		D'andalusa giovinetta
Poor young hero, brought to his knees,		Follemente innamorò;
By a proud capricious beauty:		Ma la bella ritrosetta
She was fair but hard to please.		Così al giovine parlò:

'Vanquish five young bulls for me',
She said, 'and all within a day:
If you win, then come to see me
And I'll let you have your way.
He accepted her commission;
Next day he was in the ring.
He achieved a life's ambition:
Five went down, Piquillo was King.

Cinque tori in un sol giorno
Vo' vederti ad atterrar;
E, se vinci, al tuo ritorno
Mano e cor ti vo' donar.
Si, gli disse, e il mattadore,
Alle giostre mosse il pie';
Cinque tori, vincitore,
Sull'arena egli stendé.

THE OTHERS

Bravo, bravo, young Piquillo,
What a glorious prize to gain!
Did your lady come to hail you
As the bravest hero in Spain?

Bravo, bravo il mattadore,
Ben gagliardo si mostrò,
Se alla giovane l'amore
In tal guisa egli provò.

GASTON WITH MATADORS

Cheered by all the smiling faces,
Young Piquillo claimed his bride;
He was met with sweet embraces,
He subdued her maiden pride.

Poi, tra plausi, ritornato
Alla bella del suo cor,
Colse il premio desiato
Tra le braccia dell'amor.

THE OTHERS

That's why matadors are famous,
They can win a woman's heart.

Con tai prove i mattadori
San le belle conquistar!

GASTON WITH MATADORS

Here in Paris you will tame us,
Teach us laughter for a start.

Ma qui son più miti i cori;
A noi basta folleggiar...

ALL
(*The gipsies strike their tambourines and the Picadors their pikes on the ground.*)
Yes, yes, we will teach you laughter
And the fickle smiles of chance;
Now the cards are dealt, but, after,
We'll have half the night to dance.

Si, si, allegri... Or pria tentiamo
Della sorte il vario umor;
La palestra dischiudiamo
Agli audaci giuocator.

The men take off their masks; some disperse, and some begin to play at the gaming tables.
Scene Twelve. *Enter Alfredo. Continuation of Finale two.*

ALL
Alfredo! You!

Alfredo!... Voi!...

ALFREDO
Yes, I'm back, friends.

Si, amici...

FLORA
Violetta?

Violetta?

ALFREDO
I don't know.

Non ne so.

ALL
That's how to take it! Splendid! You'll
join us in a game?

Ben disinvolto!... Bravo! Or via, giuocar
si può.

Gaston goes to the table, Alfredo and others stake money. Enter Violetta leaning on the Baron's arm. Flora goes forward to meet them. [21]

FLORA
I wasn't sure you'd join us...

Qui desiata giungi.

VIOLETTA
After your charming letter?

Cessi al cortese invito.

FLORA
Baron, you're very welcome. I am so
pleased to see you.

Grata vi son, barone, d'averlo pur gradito.

BARON
(*in an undertone to Violetta*)
Germont is here! Do you see him?

(Germont è qui! il vedete!)

VIOLETTA
(*aside*)
(God, what will happen?)

(Cielo!... gli è vero.)
(*in an undertone to the Baron*)
I see him!

Il vedo.

63

BARON
(in a dark voice)

Ignore him absolutely! You must not even greet him! You say nothing,	Da voi non un sol detto si volga a questo Alfredo.
Do you hear me?	Non un detto!

VIOLETTA
(aside) [22]

(It was madness to come here!	(Ah, perché venni, incauta!
Dear God I beg, do not forsake me now.)	Pietà, di me gran Dio; pietà di me!)

Flora invites Violetta to sit on the sofa beside her, the Doctor stands beside them; the Marquis converses apart with the Baron; Gaston cuts; Alfredo and others stake; some saunter about.

FLORA

Sit here beside me; talk to me…	Meco t'assidi; narrami…
That's a new dress you're wearing…	Quai novità vegg'io?…

(Flora and Violetta converse aside.)

ALFREDO

A seven!	Un quattro!

GASTON

You're still the winner.	Ancora hai vinto!

ALFREDO
(stakes and wins)

The poor unlucky lover Has all the luck at gambling.	Sfortuna nell'amore Vale fortuna al giuoco!…

ALL

You have had all the winners.	È sempre vincitore!…

ALFREDO

Oh I will win this evening, I'll beat whoever offers;	Oh, vincerò stasera; e l'oro guadagnato
Then I'll enjoy my gold in the country where I'm happy.	Poscia a goder tra'campi ritornerò beato.

FLORA

Alone?	Solo?

ALFREDO

Ah, no! I'll live with a woman who adored me,	No, no, con tale che vi fu meco ancor,
Then threw me over.	Poi mi sfuggia…

VIOLETTA

Alfredo!	(Mio Dio!…)

GASTON
(to Alfredo, pointing at Violetta)

(Be kind to her.)	(Pietà di lei!)

BARON
(to Alfredo, with ill-suppressed anger)

Germont!	Signor!

VIOLETTA
(in an undertone to the Baron)

(I'll leave if you make trouble.)	(Frenatevi, o vi lascio.)

ALFREDO
(carelessly)

I think I heard the Baron?	Barone, m'appellaste?

BARON
(ironically)

Since you have been so lucky, I'd like to take you on sir.	Siete in si gran fortuna, che al giuoco mi tentaste.

ALFREDO
(ironically)

Yes! I accept your challenge.	Si?… la disfida accetto…

VIOLETTA
(aside)

I long for the earth to open!	Che fia? morir mi sento!
Dear God, I beg, do not forsake me now!	Pietà, gran Dio, di me!

BARON
(stakes)

I bet one hundred louis. Cento luigi a destra.

ALFREDO
(stakes)

I bet one hundred also. Ed alla manca cento.

GASTON

An ace... a knave... the winner! Un asso... un fante... hai vinto!

BARON

Two hundred? Il doppio?

ALFREDO

The stake is doubled. Il doppio sia.

GASTON
(cutting)

A four, a seven. Un quattro, un sette.

ALL

Alfredo! Ancora!

ALFREDO

My run of luck continues! Pur la vittoria è mia!

ALL

Luck is like that! This evening it Bravo davver!... la sorte è tutta per
smiles upon Alfredo! Alfredo!

FLORA

Country expenses settled: the Baron will be Del villeggiar la spesa farà il baron, già
paying. il vedo.

ALFREDO
(to the Baron)

You'll play again? Seguite pur.

SERVANT

The supper's ready. La cena è pronta.

FLORA

I'm hungry! Andiamo.

ALL

We'll go then! Andiamo.

(They go out, leaving Alfredo and the Baron behind.)

ALFREDO
(to the Baron)

Shall we continue playing? Se continuar v'aggrada...

BARON

We must go in to supper: Per ora nol possiamo:
I'd like another round with you. Più tardi la rivincita.

ALFREDO

You choose the game, I'm ready. Al gioco che vorrete.

BARON

We'll join the others... Later! Seguiam gli amici; poscia...

ALFREDO

I'm always at your service. Sarò qual bramerete.

(Exeunt.)

ALFREDO

Lead on! Andiam.

BARON

Monsieur. Andiam.

Scene Thirteen. *Re-enter Violetta in great agitation, afterwards Alfredo.*

VIOLETTA

I have asked him here to meet me. Invitato a qui seguirmi,
Will he do so? And will he listen? Verrà desso?... vorrà udirmi?...
He will come... And yet there's nothing Ei verrà... ché l'odio atroce
I can say to quell his loathing! Puote in lui più di mia voce...

65

ALFREDO

I must ask you why you called me! / Mi chiamaste? che bramate?

VIOLETTA

You must go away this moment... / Questi luoghi abbandonate...
If you stay here you're in danger. / Un periglio vi sovrasta...

ALFREDO

Ah, I follow! you are trembling... / Ah, comprendo!...Basta,basta...
So you think that I'm a coward? / E sì vile mi credete?

VIOLETTA

Ah no, no, never! / Ah no, mai...

ALFREDO

But you are frightened? / Ma che temete?...

VIOLETTA

I am frightened that the Baron... / Temo sempre del Barone...

ALFREDO

He and I will fight a duel. / È tra noi mortal quistione...
We will fight and if I kill him, / S'ei cadrà per mano mia
With a single blow I'd rob you / Un sol colpo vi torria
Of your lover and protector... / Coll'amante il protettore...
You're afraid that you'd be ruined! / V'atterrisce tal sciagura?

VIOLETTA

What if you should be the victim? / Ma s'ei fosse l'uccisore?
That's the thing I am afraid of, / Ecco l'unica sventura...
And for me it would be fatal. / Ch'io pavento a me fatale!

ALFREDO

If he kills me—does it matter? / La mia morte!...Che ven cale?...

VIOLETTA

Leave, I beg you...ah, stay no longer! / Deh, partite, e sull'istante.

ALFREDO

I will go if you will give your word / Partirò, ma giura innante
to come with me this moment / Che dovunque seguirai
And to stay with me forever. / I miei passi...

VIOLETTA

I cannot do it. / Ah, no, giammai.

ALFREDO

What—you cannot? / No! giammai!...

VIOLETTA

You must forget me! / Va, sciagurato.
Poor Alfredo, if you stay here my dishonour / Scorda un nome ch'è infamato.
will torment you... / Va...mi lascia sul momento...
I have sworn an oath to give you up / Di fuggirti un giuramento...
for ever! / Sacro io feci...

ALFREDO

To whom? Tell me, who could force you? / E chi potea?

VIOLETTA

One who had the right to ask me. / A chi diritto pien n'aveva.

ALFREDO

Not the Baron? / Fu Douphol?...

VIOLETTA

(*with painful effort*)
Yes. / Sì.

ALFREDO

So you love him? / Dunque l'ami?

VIOLETTA

Yes, I...love him. / Ebben...l'amo...

ALFREDO

(*furiously rushing to the door*)
Come here, come here. / Or tutti a me.

Scene Fourteen. *All re-enter hurriedly.*

ALL

Why this shouting? What has happened? | Ne appellaste?... Che volete?

ALFREDO

(*pointing to Violetta, who, overwhelmed with grief, leans on a table to support herself*)
Do you recognise this woman? | Questa donna conoscete?

ALL

Who?... Violetta? | Chi?... Violetta?

ALFREDO

Have you heard her noble story? | Che facese
Non sapete? |

VIOLETTA

Be silent. | Ah, taci...

ALL

No. | No.

ALFREDO

All that she had she spent on me, | Ogni suo aver tal femmina
Only because she loved me... | Per amor mio sperdea...
A selfish coward, kept by her, | Io cieco, vile, misero,
I grasped at all she gave me. | Tutto accettar potea,
Now I can pay the debt I owe, | Ma è tempo ancora!... tergermi
Now I can clear my honour... | Di tanta macchia bramo...
I call you here to witness | Qui testimon vi chiamo
That I have paid my debt. | Che qui pagata io l'ho.

With furious disdain he throws a purse at Violetta's feet, she faints into Flora's arms. Germont enters at the same moment. **Scene Fifteen.**

ALL

You have destroyed her. | [23] Oh, infamia orribile
Our senses are reeling, | Tu commettesti!...
Are you devoid of all pity and feeling? | Un cor sensibile
He who is brutally rude to a woman | Così uccidesti!...
Must take society's curse evermore. | Di donne ignobile
Leave us, leave us for evermore! | Insultator,
| Di qui allontanati,
| Ne desti orror.

GERMONT

(*dignified, but angry*)
Disgraceful outrage! We all despise you! | Di sprezzo degno se stesso rende
You shout in anger, you shame a woman. | Chi pur nell'ira la donna offende.
My son Alfredo I see no longer. | Dov'è mio figlio?... più non lo
My only son Alfredo... I cannot see him here. | vedo:
| In te più Alfredo—trovar non
(Where is Alfredo? Where will I find him? | so.
You're not Alfredo, my son, you're not my son.) | (Io sol fra tanti so qual virtude
| Di quella misera il sen racchiude...
| Io so che l'ama, che gli è fedele,
| Eppur, crudele — tacer dovrò!)

ALFREDO

(*aside*)
Oh God forgive me! I'm like a madman! | Ah, sì... che feci!... ne sento orrore...
In jealous frenzy I shame a woman! | Gelosa smania, deluso amore
My heart is breaking, I've lost my reason, | Mi strazia l'alma... più non ragiono.
All hope of pardon is over now. | Da lei perdono—più non avrò.
I thought of leaving but when I tried it | Volea fuggirla... non ho potuto!
My anger spurred me, I couldn't hide it! | Dall'ira spinto son qui venuto!
I poured my heart out with all its venom. | Or che lo sdegno ho disfogato,
All hope of pardon is over now. | Me sciagurato!—rimorso n'ho.

VIOLETTA

(*recovering consciousness with a faint voice, but with passion*)
Alfredo, Alfredo, you hate and scorn me, | Alfredo, Alfredo, di questo core
You do not realise the bitter story... | Non puoi comprendere tutto l'amore;
How can I tell you how much I love you? | Tu non conosci che fino a prezzo
You may despise me, but I gave my word. | Del tuo disprezzo—provato io l'ho!

The time is coming when you'll discover
How I was truly your faithful lover,
And then may God in his wisdom help you,
Show you mercy, may he save you from
  remorse!
Ah, my love for you will never die.

Ma verrà giorno in che il saprai...
Com'io t'amassi confesserai...
Dio dai rimorsi ti salvi allora,
Io spenta ancora—pur t'amerò.

BARON
(in an undertone to Alfredo)

You dare insult a woman, your odious
  cruelty fills us with loathing.
But I shall punish this dreadful
  outrage;
I want to show you that I can humble
  your cursed pride.

A questa donna l'atroce insulto
Qui tutti offese, ma non inulto
Fia tanto oltraggio... provar vi voglio

Che tanto orgoglio—fiaccar saprò.

ALL

Oh poor Violetta, come, dry your eyes. [24]
We suffer with you and sympathise.
Ah, how you suffer! Try to forget it!
Dearest Violetta, we are your friends.

Oh, quanto peni!... Ma pur fa core...
Qui soffre ognuno del tuo dolore;
Fra cari amici qui sei soltanto;
Riasciuga il pianto—che t'inondò.

Germont leads off his son, followed by the Baron. The Doctor and Flora conduct Violetta away, while the others disperse.

Curtain.

Norman Bailey (Germont) with John Brecknock (Alfredo) in the ENO production by John Copley

Act Three

Prelude [1].

Scene One. *Violetta's bedroom. A bed with curtains half-drawn at the back; window closed; on a small table by the bed are a decanter with water, a glass, and various medicines. In the centre of the stage is a dressing-table, and beside it a sofa; other furniture—a nightlight is burning. There is a door to the left; a fire in the grate. Violetta discovered asleep in bed, Annina seated by the fireplace also asleep. Recitative and Aria*

VIOLETTA
(waking)

Annina?   Annina?

ANNINA
(rousing herself)

Did you call me?   Comandate?

VIOLETTA

Poor creature, were you sleeping?   Dormivi, poveretta?

ANNINA

Yes, please forgive me.   Sì, perdonate.

VIOLETTA

Let me have some water.   Dammi d'acqua un sorso.

(Annina obeys.)

The window... it must be morning?   Osserva è pieno il giorno?

ANNINA

Just gone seven.   Son sett'ore.

VIOLETTA

Let me have the curtains open.   Da' accesso a un po' di luce...

(Annina opens the window and looks out on the street.)

ANNINA

Doctor Grenville is here.   Il signor di Grenvil!...

VIOLETTA

Ah, he's so loyal!   Oh, il vero amico!...
I must get up... please help me!   Alzar mi vo'... m'aita.

She tries to rise, but fails; then supported by Annina goes slowly to the sofa; the Doctor enters in time to help her sit down. **Scene Two.**

VIOLETTA

You're very kind—thinking of me so early!   Quanta bontà... Pensaste a me per tempo!...

DOCTOR
(feeling her pulse)

Well, are you feeling better?   Sì, come vi sentite?

VIOLETTA

I feel exhausted, but my mind is calmer.   Soffre il mio copro, ma tranquilla ho l'alma.
A priest came here last evening and brought   Mi confortò iersera un pio ministro.
me comfort.
Ah, religion is the only balm to those who   Religione è sollievo a' sofferenti.
suffer.

DOCTOR

Your night was peaceful?   E questa notte?

VIOLETTA

Thank you, I slept quite calmly.   Ebbi tranquillo il sonno.

DOCTOR

Why that is splendid... That's a certain   Coraggio adunque... la convalescenza
sign that
You're getting better.   Non è lontana...

VIOLETTA

Ah, lies you tell in pity   Oh, la bugia pietosa
Are pardoned in a doctor!   A' medici è concessa...

DOCTOR
(clasping her hand)

Goodbye now, till this evening!   Addio... a' più tardi.

69

VIOLETTA

You won't forget me?   Non mi scordate.

Exit Doctor; Annina goes out with him.

ANNINA

Is she really better?   Come va, signore?

DOCTOR

She's dying of consumption, her life is over.   La tisi non le accorda che poche ore.

Scene Three.

ANNINA

Now come, take heart.   Or fate cor.

VIOLETTA

Is not today a feast day?   Giorno di festa è questo?

ANNINA

Carnival Day has started... they're all   Tutta Parigi impazza... è carnevale...
rejoicing.

VIOLETTA

Ah, but behind the laughter, God looks   Ah, nel comun tripudio, sallo il cielo...
down on
Many who weep and suffer. How much   Quanti infelici soffron!... Quale somma
money
Is left, Annina?   V'ha in quello stipo?

(pointing to her purse)

ANNINA
(opens and counts)

Just twenty louis.   Venti luigi.

VIOLETTA

Go   Dieci
And give ten to the poor folk who need it.   Ne reca ai poveri tu stessa.

ANNINA

That leaves you hardly any...   Poco
Rimanvi allora...

VIOLETTA

Oh, I've enough to last me...   Oh, mi sarà bastante;
See if a letter has come for me.   Cerca poscia mie lettere.

ANNINA

But you?   Ma voi?...

VIOLETTA

I'll be all right, but hurry back, Annina.   Nulla occorrà... sollecita, se puoi...

Exit Annina. **Scene Four.** *Violetta draws a letter from her bosom and reads.* [6]

"You have kept your promise... the duel   "Teneste la promessa... la disfida
Took place. The baron was wounded,   Ebbe luogo! il barone fu ferito,
But he is recovering... Alfredo   Però migliora... Alfredo
Has gone abroad; I have written to tell him   È in stranio suolo; il vostro sagrifizio
Of the sacrifice you made.   Io stesso gli ho svelato;
He is coming back to beg your forgiveness.   Egli a voi tornerà pel suo perdono;
I shall come too... take care of yourself.   Io pur verrò... Curatevi... mertate
You deserve a better future.   Un avvenir migliore.
Giorgio Germont."   Giorgio Germont."

VIOLETTA
(in a sepulchral voice)

Too late...   È tardi!...

(rises)

I've waited and waited... they will never   Attendo, attendo... né a me giungon
come now!...   mai!...

(looking at herself in the mirror)

How altered they would find me!   Oh, come son mutata!
Still, the doctor seemed to think I would   Ma il dottore a sperar pure m'esorta!...
recover!
Ah, I am dying! With this disease it's   Ah, con tal morbo ogni speranza è morta.
hopeless!
I've lost you, happy daydreams,   [26] Addio, del passato bei sogni ridenti,
The past is all over.

70

The roses of my young days have faded for ever.	Le rose del volto già sono pallenti;
I've lost my Alfredo, the one who could cheer me,	L'amore d'Alfredo pur esso mi manca,
My soul was sustained and refreshed when he was near me.	Conforto, sostegno dell'anima stanca...
All comfort is gone. Ah! Smile on the poor creature	Ah, della traviata sorridi al desio;
Whose life has lost its savour.	
Dear God, I now implore you to grant me this favour.	A lei, deh, perdona; tu accoglila, o Dio,
Ah, now my life is done,	Or tutto fini.
All my life is over.	
All pleasure and grieving will shortly be over;	Le gioie, i dolori tra poco avran fine,
The darkness of the graveyard will shroud me from my lover!	La tomba ai mortali di tutto è confine!
No cross with my name shall ever mark where they lay me,	Non lagrima o fiore avrà la mia fossa,
No mourners with flowers will come to bewail me!	Non croce col nome che copra quest' ossa!
Ah, smile on the creature whose life has lost its savour:	Ah, della traviata sorridi al desio;
Dear God I now implore you to grant me this favour!	A lei, deh, perdona; tu accoglila, o Dio.
Ah, now all my life is done,	Or tutto fini!
All my life is over.	

(She sits. Carnival Chorus)

CHORUS
(outside)

Hail to the carnival's	[27] Largo al quadrupede
Four-footed master!	Sir della festa,
Round him the vine leaves	Di fiori e pampini
And bright flowers cluster!	Cinto la testa...
No need to fear his horns,	Largo al più docile
He wouldn't eat you,	D'ogni cornuto,
So play your pipes and drums!	Di corni e pifferi
Ox, we all greet you.	Abbia il saluto.
So now citizens of Paris	Parigini, date passo
Step aside and own him master,	Al trionfo del Bue grasso.
The great fat Ox is master.	*(repeat)*
Yes, the great fat Ox is master!	
Asia and Africa	L'Asia, né l'Africa
Bow down and serve him:	Vide il più bello,
Ev'rywhere butchers are	Vanto ed orgoglio
Vying to carve him.	D'ogni macello...
Maskers, apprentices	Allegre maschere,
Cheer him with singing	Pazzi garzoni,
Ev'ry one pay his due	Tutti plauditelo
Till the streets are ringing.	Con canti e suoni!...
So now, citizens of Paris,	Parigini, date passo
Step aside and own him master,	Al trionfo del Bue grasso.
The great fat Ox is master,	
Yes, the great fat Ox is master!	*(repeat)*

Annina re-enters hurriedly. **Scene Five**/*Recitative and Duet*

ANNINA
(with hesitation)

Dear Madam—	Signora!

VIOLETTA

What has happened?	Che t'accade?

ANNINA

Now tell me... this morning, are you feeling better?	Quest'oggi, è vero? Vi sentite meglio?...

VIOLETTA

Yes, but why?   Sì, perché?

ANNINA

And you won't get too excited?   D'esser calma promettete?

VIOLETTA

No, why d'you ask me?   Sì, che vuoi dirmi?

ANNINA

Only to prepare you   Prevenir vi volli…
For a joy you'd ceased to hope for…   Una gioia improvvisa…

VIOLETTA

Ceased to hope for? You mean it?   Una gioia!… dicesti?…

ANNINA

God didn't fail us…   Sì, o signora…

VIOLETTA

Alfredo! You mean you've seen him? Alfredo!… Ah, tu il vedesti?…
He's here! Oh hurry!   ei vien!… l'affretta.

Scene Six. *Alfredo appears.*

Alfredo!   Alfredo!

(They embrace.)

Oh my Alfredo, my beloved, oh Alfredo, Amato Alfredo! o gioja!
oh my joy!

ALFREDO

Oh, my Violetta, my beloved, oh Violetta,   Mia Violetta! o gioja!
oh my joy.
My father told me… that dreadful meeting… Colpevol sono… so tutto, o cara.

VIOLETTA

But you are back now, you're here beside Io so che alfine reso mi sei!…
me.

ALFREDO

I'm so in love with you my heart is beating, Da questo palpito s'io t'ami impara,
And life is misery when you're not   Senza te esistere più non potrei.
with me.

VIOLETTA

If I am living and you are with me,   Ah, s'anco in vita m'hai ritrovata,
No grief in all the world can kill me now. Credi che uccidere non può il dolor.

ALFREDO

Forget your sorrow, my own beloved,   Scorda l'affanno, donna adorata,
Can you forgive my broken vow?   A me perdona e al genitor.

VIOLETTA

Can I forgive you? I too am guilty,   Ch'io ti perdoni? la rea son io;
It was for love I made my choice.   Ma solo amore tal mi rendé…

ALFREDO

Ah, neither man nor devil now   Null'uomo o demone, angelo mio,
Will dare divide us for evermore.   Mai più dividerti potrà da me.
Come, bid farewell to Paris for ever, [28] Parigi, o cara, noi lasceremo,
We will be happy living together.   La vita uniti trascorreremo:
Your grief will vanish now I'm beside you, De' corsi affanni compenso avrai,
New life will blossom, you will be well. La tua salute rifiorirà.
Your light and spirit glow here inside me: Sospiro e luce tu mi sarai,
Trust in the future, all will be well.   Tutto il futuro ne arriderà.

VIOLETTA

Ah neither man nor devil now   Null'uomo o demone, angelo mio,
Will dare divide us for evermore.   Mai più dividerti potrà da me,
I'll bid farewell to Paris for ever,   Parigi, o caro, noi lasceremo,
We will be happy living together.   La vita uniti trascorreremo:
My grief will vanish now you're beside me, De' corsi affanni compenso avrai,
New life will blossom, I shall be well. La mia salute rifiorirà.
Your light and spirit glow here inside me. Sospiro e luce tu mi sarai,
Trust in the future, all will be well.   Tutto il futuro ne arriderà.

VIOLETTA

Ah, no more, Alfredo, let's go to church Ah, non più, a un tempio… Alfredo
now,   andiamo,

Give thanks to Heaven that we're together.   Del tuo ritorno grazie rendiamo...
                                    (*faltering*)
                                    ALFREDO
You're pale and trembling!   Tu impallidisci...

                                    VIOLETTA
            No, no,   È nulla, sai!
It's nothing; I'm so excited... I've   Gioia improvvisa non entra mai
been so wretched, and now you're   Senza turbarlo in mesto core...
with me... give me a moment.

            (*Violetta sinks exhausted on a couch.*)
                                    ALFREDO
                    (*with horror, raising her*)
Violetta, what is it?   Gran Dio!... Violetta!

                                    VIOLETTA
            A touch of fainting   È il mio malore...
After my illness... Now I feel stronger...   Fu debolezza! ora son forte...
                                    (*with an effort*)
See I am smiling.   Vedi?... sorrido...
                                    ALFREDO
                        (*sorrowfully*)
            Ah, how you're suff'ring!   (Ahi, cruda sorte!...)
                                    VIOLETTA
It's nothing! Annina, help me to dress now.   Fu nulla... Annina, dammi a vestire.
                                    ALFREDO
Violetta... have patience...   Adesso?... attendi...
                                    VIOLETTA
                        (*rising*)
            No, no, I want to.   No... voglio uscire.
(*Annina gives her a garment, she begins to put it on, but faintness prevents her; she lets it fall
and exclaims despairingly.*)
Oh, God! I cannot!   Gran Dio! non posso!
                    (*She falls back on the couch.*)
                                    ALFREDO
            Dearest Violetta!   (Cielo!... che vedo!...)
                        (*to Annina*)
Go find the doctor.   Va pel dottore...
                                    VIOLETTA
                        (*to Annina*)
            Yes, fetch him,   Digli che Alfredo
Tell him Alfredo has not forgotten and that   È ritornato all'amor mio...
he loves me.
Tell him I need to be well, I want to live   Digli che vivere ancor vogl' io...
again.

                    (*Exit Annina.*)
                                    VIOLETTA
                        (*to Alfredo*)
But if your coming cannot revive me,   Ma se tornando nor m'hai salvato,
No power on earth can prevent my dying.   A niuno in terra salvarmi è dato.
                        (*rising impetuously*)
Ah! dear God, to die when I'm so young [29]   Gran Dio! morir sì giovane,
And after so much sorrow!   Io che penato ho tanto!
And now that I have come so near   Morir sì presso a tergere
The comfort I have longed for!   Il mio sì lungo pianto!
My hope of future happiness   Ah, dunque fu delirio
Was nothing but delusion!   La credula speranza;
My faith and my devotion   Invano di costanza
All a vain and empty dream.   Armato avrà il mio cor!
Alfredo dearest, oh cruel destiny   Alfredo!... oh, il crudo termine
Reserved for all our love!   Serbato al nostro amor!
                                    ALFREDO
Ah, you're the breath of life to me   Oh mio sospiro e palpito,
Violetta, my own darling.   Diletto del cor mio!...

                    73

I cannot help but weep to see	Le mie colle tue lagrime
Your tears of anguish falling.	Confondere degg'io...
Believe me, I have need of you,	Ma più che mai, deh, credilo.
Your faith and your devotion,	M'è d'uopo di constanza.
So trust in your emotion,	Ah! tutto alla speranza
We still can hope and dream.	Non chiudere il tuo cor.
Violetta darling, calm yourself!	Violetta mia, deh, calmati,
Your grieving breaks my heart.	M'uccide il tuo dolor.

Violetta sinks onto the couch. **Final Scene.** *Enter Annina, Germont and the Doctor.*

Finale

GERMONT

Ah, Violetta!   Ah, Violetta!...

VIOLETTA

You, monsieur!   Voi, Signor!...

ALFREDO

Dear father!   Mio padre!

VIOLETTA

You've not forgotten?   Non mi scordaste?

GERMONT

I have not forgotten...   La promessa adempio...

You see I keep my promise and accept you	A stringervi qual figlia vengo al seno
As a daughter!	O generosa...

VIOLETTA

Too late! you cannot help me.   Ahimè, tardi giungeste!

(embracing him)

But I thank you for coming...	Pure, grata ven sono...
You see, dear Doctor, even though I'm dying	Grenvil, vedete? tra le braccia io spiro
My dearest friends are with me.	Di quanti ho cari al mondo...

GERMONT

(gazing at Violetta)

No, it can't be!   Che mai dite!

(to himself)

(Oh Heaven! It's true!)   (Oh cielo... è ver!)

ALFREDO

Oh father, do you see her?   La vedi, padre mio?

GERMONT

My son do not torment me.	Di più non lacerarmi...
I now reproach myself for what has	Troppo rimorso l'alma mi divora...
happened...	
Ev'ry word that she utters scorches like	Quasi fulmin m'atterra ogni suo detto...
lightning...	
I should never have spoken!	Oh, malcauto vegliardo!
I understand now how I destroyed her!	Ah, tutto il mal ch'io feci ora sol vedo!

(Violetta opens a casket and takes a medallion out of it.)

VIOLETTA

Come close beside me, beloved, my dear	Più a me t'appressa... ascolta, amato
Alfredo...	Alfredo.
Listen! I have a picture here	Prendi; quest'è l'immagine
Of me when I was younger:	De' miei passati giorni;
By this you will remember	A rammentar ti torni
How much I was in love.	Colei che si t'amò,
I see a pure and lovely girl, [30]	Se una pudica vergine
Fair as a flower in springtime,	Degli anni suoi nel fiore
Offering her devotion...	A te donasse il core...
And you will marry, yes, make her your	Sposa ti sia... lo vo'.
wife.	
Give her this little portrait,	Le porgi questa effigie:
Tell her it is a gift	Dille che dono ell'è
From someone in eternity,	Di chi nel ciel tra gli angeli
Praying for her and you.	Prega per lei, per te.

ALFREDO

No, do not die, don't talk like that,	No, non morrai, non dirmelo...
For you must live my darling.	Dêi viver, amor mio...

God wouldn't be so cruel	A strazio sì terribile
To bring me here to suffer.	Qui non mi trasse Iddio...
You cannot leave me now,	Sì presto, ah no, dividerti
Death cannot take you now away from me.	Morte non può da me.
But if you will not stay with me	Ah, vivi, o un solo feretro
I want to die with you.	M'accoglierà con te.

GERMONT

Beloved daughter, your noble	Cara, sublime vittima
Sacrifice has covered you with glory,	D'un disperato amore,
Forgive me for the torment	Perdonami lo strazio
I caused your noble heart.	Recato al tuo bel core.

GERMONT, DOCTOR AND ANNINA

As long as eyes have tears to weep,	Finché avrà il ciglio lacrime
I'll weep for you.	Io piangerò per te.
You go to join the spirits,	Vola a' beati spiriti;
For God is calling you.	Iddio ti chiama a sé.

VIOLETTA
(*re-awakening*)

Alfredo!...   È strano!...

ALL

Ah!   Che!

VIOLETTA

The pain has gone... the pain has gone... [6]	Cessarono
I can breathe now. My pulse is beating.	Gli spasmi del dolore.
I feel it. Look at me.	In me rinasce... m'agita
My strength is coming back!	Insolito vigore!
Ah! why yes, I feel my life returning...	Ah, io ritorno a vivere...
What joy!	Oh gio... ia!

(*She collapses on the sofa.*)

ALL

Violetta. No!   O cielo!... muor!

ALFREDO

Violetta!   Violetta!

ANNINA AND GERMONT

Oh God receive her soul.   Oh, Dio, soccorrasi...

DOCTOR
(*after feeling her pulse*)

It's over!   È spenta!

ALL

Oh grant her rest!   Oh mio dolor!

Curtain.

Amelita Galli-Curci in the last scene
of 'La Traviata' at the Met..
(Ida Cook Collection)

75

Discography Recordings currently available in the UK and the USA in order of UK release. All performanes in stereo (unless asterisked*) and in Italian (unless †). Cassette tape numbers are also listed. A valuable review of all performances on record by Alan Blyth is included in *Opera on Record* (ed. Alan Blyth, Hutchinson 1979).

Conductor	*Panizza*	*Ghione*	*Serafin*	*Pritchard*
Company/Orchestra	New York Met. Op. Orch. & Chorus	Lisbon San Carlos Op. Orch. & Chorus	Rome Opera Orch. & Chorus	Maggio Musicale Orch. & Chorus
Date	1935	1958	1959	1962
Violetta	R. Ponselle	M. Callas	V. de los Angeles	J. Sutherland
Alfredo	F. Jagel	A. Kraus	C. del Monte	C. Bergonzi
Germont	L. Tibbett	M. Sereni	M. Sereni	R. Merrill
Flora	E. Vettori	L. Zannini	S. Chissari	M. Truccato-Pace
UK LP Number	—	EMI EX 291315-3 (2)	CFP D414450-3 (2)	—
UK Tape Number	—	EMI EX 291315-5 (2)	CFP D414450-5 (2)	—
UK CD Number	Pavilion GEMM CD9317 (2)*	EMI CDS 749187-8 (2)	—	Decca 411 877-2 (2)
US LP Number	—	EMI EX 291315-3 (2)	—	—
US Tape Number	—	EMI EX 291315-5 (2)	—	—
US CD Number	—	EMI CDS 749187-8 (2)	—	Decca 411 877-2 (2)

	Votto	Prêtre	Kleiber
Conductor			
Company	La Scala Orch. & Chorus	RCA Italiana Orch. & Chorus	Bavarian State Opera Orch. & Chorus
Date	1963	1967	1977
Violetta	R. Scotto	M. Caballé	I. Cotrubas
Alfredo	G. Raimondi	C. Bergonzi	P. Domingo
Germont	E. Bastianini	S. Milnes	S. Milnes
Flora	G. Tavolaccini	D. Krebill	S. Malagu
UK LP Number	DG 415 392-1GX2 (2)	—	—
UK Tape Number	DG 415 392-4GX2 (2)	—	—
UK CD Number	—	RCA RD86180 (2)	DG 415 132-2GH2 (2)
US LP Number	—	—	—
US Tape Number	—	—	—
US CD Number	—	RCA 6180-2RC (2)	DG 415 132-2GH2 (2)

	Bonynge	Mackerras	Muti
Conductor	*Bonynge*	*Mackerras*	*Muti*
Company	**National PO**	**ENO Orch. & Chorus**	**Philharmonia Ambrosian Op. Chorus**
Date	*1979*	*1981*	*1982*
Violetta	J. Sutherland	V. Masterson	R. Scotto
Alfredo	L. Pavarotti	J. Brecknock	A. Kraus
Germont	M. Managuerra	C. du Plessis	R. Bruson
Flora	D. Jones	D. Jones	S. Walker
UK LP Number	–	–	–
UK Tape Number	–	–	–
UK CD Number	Decca 410 154-2DH3 (3)	EMI CMS 7630722 (2)	EMI CDS 7475388 (2)
US LP Number	–	–	–
US Tape Number	–	–	–
US CD Number	Decca 410 154-2LH3 (3)	EMI CMS 7630722 (2)	EMI CDS 7475388 (2)

Excerpts

Number	Artist(s)	CD Number	LP Number	Tape Number
Preludes (Acts One and Three)	Vienna PO/Sinopoli	Philips 411 469-2PH	—	—
Prelude (Act One)	Berlin PO/Karajan	DG 423 218-2GMW	—	—
Brindisi/Un di felice/Parigi o cara	Sutherland/Pavarotti	Decca 400 058-2DH	—	—
Un di felice/Parigi o cara	Galli-Curci/Schipa	Pavilion GEMM CD9322	—	—
È strano . . . Sempre libera	Galli-Curci	Pavilion GEMM CD9308	—	—
È strano . . . Sempre libera	Te Kanawa	CBS MK37298	CBS 37298	CBS 4037298
È strano . . . Sempre libera	Sutherland	Decca 414 450-2DH2	Decca 414 450-1DH2	—
Lungi da lei . . . De' miei bollente	Domingo (Milnes cond.)	RCA RD70202	—	—
Lungi da lei . . . De' miei bollente	Domingo (C. Kleiber cond.)	DG 415 366-2GH	—	DG 419 091-4GW
Lungi da lei . . . De' miei bollente	Gigli	Pavilion GEMM CD9316	—	—
Lungi da lei . . . De' miei bollente	Wunderlich (in German)	EMI CDC 747685-2	EMI EX290988-3	—
Di Provenza il mar	Weikl	Acanta ACAN 43327	—	—
Di Provenza il mar	Fischer-Dieskau	—	—	Decca 417 340-4DA
Addio del passato	Vaness	Nixa NIXC1	Nixa NIX1	Nixa 4NIXH1

Highlights from the Bonynge set are also available on Decca CD: 400 057-2DH.

Bibliography

The chapter about *La Traviata* in Julian Budden's *The Operas of Verdi* (vol. 2 Cassell 1978) is part of his 3 volume study of all the operas and is probably the most distinguished piece of Verdi scholarship in any language. Other discussions of the opera may be found in Vincent Godefroy's *The dramatic genius of Verdi* (Gollancz, 1977) and Gabriele Baldini's *The Story of Giuseppe Verdi* (Cambridge University Press, 1980).

Budden's volume in the Master Musicians series (Dent, 1985) is an excellent study of Verdi's whole output, and D.R.B. Kimbell's *Verdi in the Age of Italian Romanticism* (Cambridge, 1981) is an invigorating study of the background and the sources of the operas.

There are classic biographies by Francis Toye *Giuseppe Verdi, His Life and Works* (Heinemann, 1931) and Frank Walker *The Man Verdi* (Dent, 1962) in which many points have been superceded by modern research. Charles Osborne's edition of *The Letters of Giuseppe Verdi* (Gollancz, 1971) is the only English translation. The Letters together with William Weaver's *Verdi: A documentary study* (Thames and Hudson, 1977) give many fascinating insights into Verdi's career. Joseph Wechsberg's *Verdi* (Weidenfeld & Nicholson, 1974), Paul Hume's *Verdi, The Man and his Music* (Hutchinson, 1978) and Charles Osborne's *Verdi* (Macmillan, 1978) also contain many superb illustrations.

The play may be read (in French) in the Clarendon French Series (General Editor W.D. Howarth) in an edition by Roger Clark, where he has written the fascinating introduction (Oxford University Press, 1972). An English version by Edith Reynolds and Nigel Playfair, *Camille*, was reprinted by Drama Books, 1957. Edmund Gosse's translation of the novel (first published in 1902) was reprinted by Corgi Books, 1959. The splendid biography of Dumas (and his father and grandfather) by André Maurois is highly recommended: *Les Trois Dumas* (Hachette, 1957), translated as *Three Musketeers* (1957).

A beautifully illustrated and well-researched study of the subject in fact and fiction has been published in France: *Les Dames aux Camélias, de l'histoire à la légende* by Christiane Issartel (Chêne Hachette, 1981).